Mel Krantzler

Learning to LOVE Again

PERENNIAL LIBRARY

Harper & Row, Publishers, New York
Cambridge, Philadelphia, San Francisco, Washington
London, Mexico City, São Paulo, Singapore, Sydney

To Pat Biondi Krantzler

The first chapter of this book originally appeared in *Cosmopolitan* in somewhat different form.

A hardcover edition of this book was originally published in 1977 by Thomas Y. Crowell Company.

First PERENNIAL LIBRARY edition published 1987.

Library of Congress Cataloging-in-Publication Data

Krantzler, Mel.
  Learning to love again.

  "Perennial Library."
  Includes index.
  1. Divorces.   2. Interpersonal relations.
3. Intimacy (Psychology)   4. Remarriage.   I. Title.
HQ814.K73   1987   301.42′84   77-6347
ISBN 0-06-097100-2 (pbk.)

89 90 91 MPC 10 9 8 7 6 5 4 3 2

Acknowledgments

To the members of my Learning to Love Again Seminars,
whose personal experiences, so openly and courageously
shared, made this book possible; to Dr. Seymour Boorstein,
who extended my horizons; to Ed La Rocque, friend and
critic, who offered many helpful suggestions; to my editor,
Nick Ellison, whose dedication to my project transformed a
gleam in my mind into the physical reality that is this book; to
Emily Berleth for her superb technical assistance; to Al and
Jo Hart for their positive reinforcement—my thanks.

And last, but most, to Patricia Biondi Krantzler: Lover,
friend, collaborator, critic, nurturer, separate person and
wife. This book in every way is as much her creation as it is
my own.

Mel Krantzler
San Rafael, California

Contents

Introduction: Beyond Creative Divorce

Seven years ago I joined the ranks of twenty million other divorced men and women in our country who were trying to shape new lives for themselves. I was totally unprepared for the explosive emotional realities of the first year of my divorce experience. Later I found out that I was not alone but one of millions in the divorced community who were living in the same kind of stunned disarray as I was.

Out of my experience as a human being in pain and my professional experience as a counselor in human relations, I established Creative Divorce Seminars in colleges for people like myself who wished to *learn* from their past in order to improve the quality of their present life. To "create" means to make something new—to put to effective use the inborn abilities each of us possesses in the form of intelligence, capacity for survival and risk-taking, and ability to transform self-defeating habits into constructive behavior. A "creative" divorce, therefore, meant opening up the possibility that divorce could be more than just an ending, a downhill slide to nowhere: It could also be an opportunity to create a new beginning for oneself.

My Creative Divorce Seminars, which I established on the West Coast in 1971, were designed primarily to help people like myself who were in the early throes of the divorce experience, the men and women who were separated or divorced for less than two years. My book *Creative Divorce: A New Opportunity for Personal Growth*, published in 1974, shared the results of my work and was written to help people when they needed help the most—when things were falling apart inside and outside themselves during the early stages of their divorce.

But what happens to the people who have pretty well come to terms with their divorce after two or three years of living a single life, the people who have used the trauma of their divorce experience to grow from a half person into a whole person? *The need for "something more" begins to enter their lives.* This was best expressed by Janet, a woman in her mid-thirties, who recently told me in a half-apologetic way: "You know, I've been divorced three and a half years and it no longer bothers me—that's truly in the past now. My life is in pretty good shape. I like my job—I'm a department store advertising manager—and my kids aren't hassling me like they did. They've accepted our new life and we really enjoy each other. I've made a number of good new friends, so I can't say I'm lonely. I've had some short-term affairs, which sort of dribbled away even though the sex was very pleasurable. But something seems to be happening to me recently. I'm beginning to feel as if there is a real lack in my life; it's sort of like a dull ache inside that won't go away. What I'm saying is that I'm number two or three with lots of people, but what I also want to be is Number One with just one person. But that seems like a hopeless wish."

Janet's remarks struck a chord of remembrance in me. She seemed to feel just like I had felt in the third year of my divorce. The pieces of my life, by that time, had been formed into a newer and brighter pattern. However, that same push of feeling Janet was experiencing suddenly began to demand attention inside me: A shiny, look-to-the-future kind of feeling that had funny-peculiar, anxiety-ridden, apologetic overtones surrounding it. And the "dull ache" seemed to deaden the glistening promise of that need to experience a new kind of relationship, a trustworthy, unique, intimate relationship with one special person of the opposite sex—a lasting love relationship.

What I subsequently learned from my own experience (and what Janet is currently learning) is that this feeling of "a real lack" in one's life meant I was ready to open myself up to the possibility of loving and being loved again. It was the beginning of a new beginning for me, which led from the hope to the reality. And since I am no more and no less a human being than anyone else on this planet, I know my experiences are more frequently the rule than the exception for the many, many other men and women who have faced the same dilemmas and struggled toward the same solutions. This book you are reading is being written for people like Janet and the person I was—for you men and women who are beginning to feel the want and need of a special love relationship in your life and yet may be conflicted and confused about acknowledging that want and need to yourself and others. You also may be sensing a readiness in yourself to experience a profoundly satisfying intimacy, yet somehow believe intimacy may be unattainable.

It is no accident that this desire for a trustworthy love relationship edges toward the center stage in our lives *after* the first years of our divorce. For this new readiness inside ourselves for a mature, intimate connection with a person of the opposite sex is the natural *next* step in our growth as human beings. This desire for love is quite different from the poisonous needs so many of us felt in the first two years of our divorce—the need to be needed because you feel you are worthless. The need to get married again immediately for the sake of the children or for economic security or to end loneliness or to satisfy the desire for decent home cooking. And the need to convince ourselves that this mixture of desperation is "love" when we meet a presentable-looking person who might prove to be a willing receptacle for our impossible demands. Nor can a mature desire for love blossom in those of us who believe in the initial stages of divorce that love is a betrayal of ourself, a snare, and a delusion. At that time we are experiencing the overwhelming pain of love turned sour and are convinced that any and all attempts to love again will inevitably lead to a new curdling of our soul.

The recently divorced people who jump quickly into pseudo-intimate relationships out of a fear that they cannot survive alone—and the others who lock the door to the possibility of establishing new, authentically intimate relationships out of a fear that they will be "destroyed" again— are mirror-images of each other. They need the space and time and self-understanding that is necessary to fertilize the barren soil inside themselves. The fertilizer for that soil is freely available for all who wish to obtain it, as I demonstrated in *Creative Divorce*. It is learning to accept the fact that each and every one of us is a person of value and competence in our own right. It is experiencing the reality that we can connect with, love, and trust our capacities to survive in this world as sensitive, caring, capable human beings.

To learn to love ourself, perhaps for the first time in our life, is to end one vital and necessary stage in our development and to begin a new stage in our growth. It is the precondition for learning to love others again and learning to love in new ways.

When we reach this stage we find it is both an ending and a beginning. It is an end to our own false belief that we are not decent and capable persons in our own right. And it is a beginning of our realization that we have the capacity to love and be loved again by others and want and need that kind of love. Small wonder the well of mixed feelings (the sense of being pushed and pulled and empty and anxious all at the same time) that stirs inside of us! New adventures in life are awaiting us and we simmer with uncertainty over the dangers as well as the opportunities that perhaps are lurking around the next corner of our life.

Yet deep inside us, we know that what we want is right for us and that no apology or denial is needed. It is neither shameful nor hopeless, neither fairy-tale fantasy nor romantic foolishness to acknowledge the desire to reach out and love again. The healthy part of ourself is searching for a special kind of enriching fulfillment that is not afforded by other options in life, no matter how valuable those other options may be.

It is no accident that four out of five divorced men and women eventually remarry, and more than one million of them each year make that choice. Dr. Helen Singer Kaplan says:

> Most people would probably be happiest in a gentle, committed, intimate relationship that is also sexually satisfying. I think human beings are a bonding species —not all species are. Some species bond for only half an hour during the mating season; others, for a lifetime. We have no way of knowing what our natural bonding pattern is—what we are actually programmed for— because economic and social pressures have always demanded lifetime bonding. . . .
>
> I've seen people happy together for a lifetime. I have also seen people who tired of one another after three or four years. I don't know the answer. But my guess— and it is only a guess—would be that most people are comfortable as married couples.*

The disturbing world you and I live in, by negative example, validates our desire for fulfillment and growth through a loving relationship. We all feel a lack of trust in our society's leaders and institutions. Who and what can we count on? Instability is king when a stable job might disappear next week or next month and the prices in the supermarket won't even remain the same next week. Hypocrisy, lies, ripoffs, double-talk, and double standards seem to be the

---

*Dr. Helen Singer Kaplan, "Sexual Freedom or Remarriage or . . . ," *Harper's Bazaar*, July 1976, p. 96c.

only certain definition of our times—all combining to create a sense of isolation, disorientation, victimization, and powerlessness inside us. But feeling every person is an enemy until he or she proves otherwise makes us less than human. Distrust, apathy, hate, frustration, and bitterness are qualities that will starve and destroy us if we allow them to be our daily bread. It is no solution to become the evil we react against. To allow that to happen violates the desire for positive growth that inheres in each of us from the time we were born to the time we die. We want to become more human rather than less, as Bertolt Brecht writes in a favorite poem of mine:

On my wall hangs a Japanese carving,
The mask of an evil demon, decorated with gold lacquer.
Sympathetically I observe
The swollen veins of the forehead, indicating
What a strain it is to be evil.

The disarray in our society is telling each of us that when we lose our faith in the values we have lived by but have taken for granted, life becomes less than bearable. We may never have concerned ourselves with how much we need trust and stability, honesty and dependability, self-respect and respect for others, commitment and love in our lives until these values were almost bludgeoned to death by Watergate, Vietnam, depression, and big-brother government. I see this jolt to our complacency as a healthy learning experience because it has forced us to realize that a life lived without these values is little more than a vegetable existence.

In today's world these basic human values rightfully

assume paramount importance in our lives, since they are the means by which we can prevent the menacing forces in our society from transforming us into ciphers without the will to improve the quality of our lives. Each of us has the potential to live the reality of these values because they reside within us; they are as much a part of who we are as the heartbeat in our chest. If society is attacking these values, we can build a fortress within ourselves to withstand the attack by taking as our starting point that which we have the power to do something positive about, namely ourselves. For we can improve our understanding of ourselves. Our greater understanding of ourselves then enables us to change our reactions to the world around us, the way we relate to ourselves and others, and in doing so change our personal world for the better.

Nowhere is the truth of these statements more in evidence than in the lives of those of us who have experienced divorce. We find ourselves, after the earlier painful years of separation, surviving effectively in ways we had never thought possible, proving in practice to ourselves and others that we are separate individuals of value and capability. However, after that proving-time takes place, something else happens. It is the "something else" that happened to Janet and to me—the emergence of the need for something more in our lives. And that need is for a monogamous love relationship, a need that has nothing to do with our divorce as such. But it has everything to do with the next stage in our growth as human beings. For it is through this kind of love that the values that create vitality and promise in our life can flourish. Trust and stability, honesty and dependability, self-respect and respect for others, commitment and caring, all become possible in a sharing love relationship.

However, this need is a blessing that comes in strange

disguises for the divorced because it opens us up once again to the possibility of pain, vulnerability, rejection, and the loss of personal identity. Indeed I found that I had opened up an unexpected Pandora's box of anxiety-provoking feelings. Arguments that were trying to protect me from scary feelings of vulnerability kept racing through my head. Perhaps you too have heard or are hearing those arguments inside yourself. They go like this: *Why take the risk of loving again since the last time that happened the relationship ended like an open wound? To love again would mean more pain, since loving deeply is a loser's game. Living together means being swallowed up, devoured or dissolved, doesn't it? Besides, where is there a person around to love? The chances of meeting someone are less than zero. And if by some miracle, meeting that someone should happen, the love couldn't last. Everything ends in game-playing manipulation or apathy. Better by far to close the lid on the Pandora's box of love....*

I recall that at that time those arguments sounded inside me as if they were true, but even so I couldn't quite believe them. For no matter how plausible they seemed, they also felt curiously unpersuasive, cold, and discomfiting. I felt they led to a dead end, for they buried hope and possibility in my life. I was killing off a part of myself, indeed the best part of myself, when I denied the possibility that loving and being loved might enter my life again.

Since I believe that every person (and that includes myself and you who are reading this chapter) has the power to change and grow for the better at any time in life, regardless of age, I refused to let those negative arguments dead-end my life. The reason I am writing this book is because I believe that you too may be searching for positive rather than negative solutions. If you feel you want "something more" in your life, you are quite right in being unwilling to settle for something less. For it is possible and realistic to learn to love again *in new ways*. And it is possible and realistic for you to use that new knowledge to reach out, find, and experience a profoundly satisfying love relationship. This book explores these possibilities in detail. They are possibilities I had to learn in my own personal life.

Three years after my own divorce my need to love again surfaced inside myself and clashed with those arguments that counseled hopelessness. The way I resolved those arguments in favor of taking the risk of learning to love again and meeting, living with, and then marrying a woman named Patricia Biondi, who had experienced divorce after an eighteen-year marriage, is explored in this book. Pat and I found that we felt the same needs, hopes, desires, fears, and hesitations that thousands of other divorced people continue to feel and don't quite know how to handle, just as we didn't know at the start of our relationship.

As a result of our experiences, and because I am also a divorce adjustment counselor, I began to find that an overwhelming need exists among other not-so-recently divorced men and women for help in dealing with this new development in their lives. They want to advance to the *next* stage in their lives, now that their divorce has been resolved in their feelings, and yet may feel blocked, frustrated, or at a dead end inside themselves. I therefore established Learning to Love Again Seminars three years ago at my Creative Divorce National Counseling Center to work with these people, just as I had previously established Creative Divorce Seminars to work with the recently divorced. In these new seminars, in which my wife and I are co-leaders, the not-so-recently divorced learn how to make fresh starts and to put into practice constructively their desire to learn to love again. In each of these seminars, six men and six women gather together and share their experiences in ten one-and-a-half-hour sessions. They come from all walks of life and their ages range from the middle twenties to the early sixties. They are the people who say at the start of these seminars that they can't find a special person to love, trust, and respect; that they feel frightened about loving again; that they have recently been involved in a living-together arrangement or a remarriage that turned sour; that they back away from an intimate relationship; that each new relationship seems to start off on the wrong foot. But they all agree that they want that ''something more'' in their lives that will make their lives more fulfilling and meaningful, and they are searching for ways in which to turn this hope into a reality.

This book is the product of these seminar experiences. In this book you will find the real-life stories, conflicts, dilemmas, and resolutions of people, including myself and my wife, Pat, who may have been in the same place inside themselves that you may be now. Many have taken one step further and I am writing this book in the hope that the perspective, ideas, suggestions, and guidelines it presents can be of personal help to you in taking that one step further.

As a not-so-recently divorced person you have found you are rich in resources for self-renewal in the way you have survived and come to terms with your divorce. But beyond the creative resolution of divorce problems lies a whole new world of challenges and opportunities which await you for the taking. Now is the time to once again put to use your capacity for making constructive changes, this time in response to your expanding desire to allow yourself to experience a reentry of commitment, sharing, intimacy, and love in your life.

The progress you will make toward establishing a stable

love relationship will be dependent, to a major extent, on your recognition of the route that leads to such a relationship. Taking that route involves your coming to an awareness that there are four stages to learning to love again which not-so-recently divorced people experience. The living through of one stage sets in motion the possibility of progressing to the next and higher stage. However, whether or not you progress depends on your ability to identify the traps, detours, and signposts along the route of your journey. This book will present you with a detailed understanding of these four stages which I have identified as The Remembered-Pain Stage, The Questing-Experimental Stage, The Selective-Distancing Stage, and The Creative-Commitment Stage.

Each of you will respond to this new challenge to love again in your own unique way. I hope, however, that you will see something of yourself in the experiences of myself, my wife, and the many members of my Learning to Love Again Seminars that appear in this book. The perspective and guidelines you will find in the following chapters are not limited in application to the not-so-recently divorced. It is my hope that people in fundamentally sound marriages that need revitalization—as well as people who are single, widowed, or remarried—will derive equal help from this book.

I see this book as a sharing experience, with you sharing yourself with the issues and people I am writing about. In the process we both, perhaps, can enrich each other's life. And since I am asking you to share, I must take the first step. The starting point, then, begins in the next chapter which tells my personal story of how I began to learn to love again.

1 Learning to Love Again

Pat (the woman I married four years ago) and I met at a time when we both felt our lives were at a dead end, believing in the impossibility of improving our relationships with anyone of the opposite sex, yet wanting to do so. It was at a trim-the-tree Christmas party we each almost didn't go to. I had been separated from my first wife for over seven months; after a period of six months or so of frantic, expensive, and ultimately exhausting dating activity, I had begun to look for something more satisfying. I wanted to get close to a woman. Laura, let's call her, I thought was the answer to my dreams. She was roughly my age, divorced like me, a lawyer, and with an interest in literature, music, art, and drama that I had always looked for in a woman. She loved to discuss ideas, a quality I had always liked in women since (as I later learned) it meant we didn't have to deal with the less tidy, more frightening world of feelings. After going out with her for almost a month, I convinced myself that she was the woman for me. Fantasies of having found the right mate, of a future free from loneliness danced in my head—and when she gave me the boot (nicely enough) less than two weeks before Christmas, I was desolated.

Feeling terribly sorry for myself, I spent the next five days holed up at home in the evenings, watching too much television, but also meditating on my patterns of behavior with Laura and with all the other women I had been seeing. Meditating along these lines was something I had never done before. It wasn't something I wanted to do; rather it seemed thrust on me because I was hurting and didn't know how to get rid of my pain. My previous approach to pain was to try to run away from it—get out of the apartment, see a movie, go to the neighborhood bar, meet another woman. But this time I knew from too much past experience that that method was terribly unsatisfying. So how could that method help me now? Listening to myself in the stillness I began to see that if I were ever going to achieve the kind of close relationship with a woman I wanted, I was going to have to do some changing. Not just my approach, but my whole attitude toward other people. I came on too strong, I didn't give Laura space to be herself. In fact, to me she wasn't a separate person at all, only an extension of my need to be taken care of. These weren't pleasant truths, because I was beginning to realize that they were true for my relationships with every woman who was or had been important in my life. They were in one sense reluctant truths: A part of me recognized them as valid, but most of me sought to deny them. I wasn't ready to live out the full meaning of what I had discovered about myself then. All I knew was that I was bored and disgruntled. I was no longer in the divorce crisis; that had passed. All I wanted was to wallow in self-pity. Nobody loved me, and I would be alone during the holidays and probably forever.

Under these circumstances, the invitation from an old friend to come to her trim-the-tree party was an unwelcome intrusion. I wanted her to sympathize with my pain and agree that I had a right to suffer. Instead, she told me there would be a number of interesting single women there, including a nurse she "knew" was just right for me. Here was an opportunity to try something new, to put my self-awareness to some use, and I resented it. My God, I thought, it's just not worth the effort; they will all be boring, unattractive, or attached to someone else. Who needs the agony of being turned down again? I was predicting the future as if it could only be a repetition of my past experience.

Nevertheless, by the afternoon of the party I had worked myself into such a state of exasperated self-disgust that taking the risk of going to the party and being disappointed seemed less unpleasant than continuing to sit at home and stew in my own juice. Not much, but a little. So, believing I knew full well what I would find, I got dressed and went— more out of being bored with boredom than anything else. Once there, I greeted my hostess, took a quick look around the room, and had my fears confirmed: The same bunch of boring people trying to make sophisticated small talk. Not for me, thank you, so I made a beeline for the kitchen, fortified myself with a strong drink, and took a seat away from everybody in the corner of the room next to the Christmas tree, where I could survey the crowd and keep my distance.

My eyes landed on an attractive woman sitting on the couch across the room, and I roused myself from my sour reverie long enough to consider talking to her, but then I saw the telltale flash of gold on her left hand, and immediately thought, "Wouldn't you know it, already married. Another one of those boring suburban housewives. Her husband must be in the other room." If she hadn't picked that moment to come over to the tree and ask me to help her hang some ornaments, I probably never would have made any attempt to talk to the woman who was eventually to become my wife.

Joined in the mindless task of putting little gold ornaments on someone else's Christmas tree, I soon found myself talking with her in a livelier manner than I would have thought possible. Her name was Pat, she said, and she had been divorced for a little more than a year after an eighteen-year marriage. This was the first party she had attended since she and her husband had separated; she almost didn't come, but remembered her promise to the hostess to help her with the party arrangements. She also couldn't stand the thought of being alone at Christmas. We talked about how difficult holidays were for divorced people, and she began to tell me a little about her present life. The company she worked for was about to go bankrupt, and she was afraid she would have to go on welfare; she was so far behind in her house payments that the bank was threatening to foreclose on the mortgage; she seemed to spend most of her time in the high school counselor's office trying to find out why her two teen-age daughters kept cutting classes. And to top everything off, her dog was in heat and had so excited the other dogs in the neighborhood that they were tearing her front door loose from its hinges. As she finished her tale of woe, she burst out laughing. I can still remember her laughter, and her saying, "God knows, I might as well laugh. It's better than crying." Yet, while she laughed there were tears streaming down her face. Here was a woman committed to the struggle to survive. It was her pain and her struggle to overcome it that connected with something inside myself, because I was experiencing the very same thing. I had found a person who had hit bottom and learned that she could survive. She was unaffected, open, honest, and I sensed a woman who had gone far beyond the social man-woman games we all play.

Our emotions formed a common bond at that first meeting, not the patter of "Did you see this movie?" or "What did you think of such-and-such a book?" that was my usual get-acquainted gambit. In fact, we didn't once talk that evening about the current intellectual scene nor about the college I assumed she had graduated from—information I always had thought was so important. Without realizing it, I was beginning a relationship on a more satisfying basis. By letting myself respond to her from parts of myself that had long been buried, I was laying the groundwork for the kind of relationship I was really looking for. In spite of my week's meditation, I wasn't aware of any of this at the time. All I knew was that I felt comfortable with her in a way I hadn't experienced with another woman before and I didn't know why.

LETTING GO OF OLD WAYS

I would like to report that our first real date, the following week, was successful but it wasn't. When I walked her to her car after the Christmas party, I had gotten her phone number, made some standard sexual overture which she firmly declined, and said good-night. Later in the week I called and we met for dinner at a restaurant in the building where I had an office. Things went badly from the start. As I steered the conversation to my usual topics—politics, the arts, literature—I discovered with discomfort a woman who had little interest in or knowledge of such matters, who as it happened had gone to college for only one year. During dinner a friend stopped by our table, and I remember feeling acutely ill at ease at being seen with this woman who only a few days earlier I had found so attractive, so real, so much in tune with how I felt. Now, suddenly, I took a good look at her across the table and found her momentarily unattractive. Here she was, engaged in a lively conversation with my friend, telling him about her father's experiences as one of the construction workers who had built the Golden Gate Bridge, while I squirmed with embarrassment at being seen in the company of such an unsophisticated woman. My heart sank as I wondered what in the world she and I could ever have in common. What the hell was I, who called myself an intellectual, doing with a woman like her?

After dinner, things took a turn for the worse, if that was possible. I took her to a local bar famous for its literary clientele; it was a place where I had spent many hours trading intellectual gossip with a small circle of regulars. She was, as I had already realized she would be at some level of my consciousness, completely out of her element. My whispered asides identifying this or that famous novelist or screenwriter met with blank stares. I was trying to impress her with a world that was so important to me, and she was completely oblivious to all of it! The emotional connection we had formed at the Christmas party seemed to vanish in the sound of my own voice and her answering silences. We parted company early, in the garage where she had left her car. We both knew things had gone badly; it was Pat, however, who risked broaching the subject. She asked me before we parted what kind of a relationship I was interested in, and I told her one that was open, feeling, and down-to-earth. She agreed. But somehow the way we had gotten along that evening seemed to contradict my assertions. What I said I wanted seemed to be an impossible dream and we left each other without discussing meeting again. I drove home in despair, wondering how in the world I was ever going to find a woman I could get close to and questioning whether the effort was worth it. I knew quite clearly what I didn't want; I had learned from my divorce that I had to try to be as authentic a person as I had it in my power to be. I was determined not to play games any more, but that was all I seemed to know how to do. There was a strong thrust within me to rid myself of self-defeating behavior patterns, and yet when it got down to cases I knew no other ways. I had made a connection with Pat based on our common pain and struggle, but in attempting to further that connection I had fallen back into old patterns. I really thought as I drove home depressed that evening that I was destined to lead a solitary life, a life I didn't want but which was all I could expect.

As Pat later told me, that first date was a self-confrontation for her as well. "When I left that evening I felt shaky and depressed, as if I had failed some test I knew nothing about. Fifteen minutes after we met in the restaurant I wondered what I was doing out with you. The warm, understanding man I had met at the party seemed to have turned into an intellectual snob. I remember wishing for just a moment that I could play that game, but then I got angry inside. I was tired of my own past ways of relating, of being the cute little clown, of getting approval by being funny and coming on dumb. There were so many other things inside me struggling to get out, I couldn't waste my time with anyone who wouldn't let them happen. I was attracted to you, and I hoped we might get to know each other, but I just couldn't face a relationship in which I couldn't be myself. I knew what you were thinking of me; that's why I asked you in the garage what you were really after. I wondered on the way home if we'd ever see each other again. But I decided that if we couldn't start from how we had felt at the Christmas party, there was no hope for us. I hadn't gone through all that pain of my divorce just to fit myself into some man's image of what a woman should be. I had to find out who I was.''

PROCEEDING AT YOUR OWN PACE

Obviously, we didn't break things off that evening. With more than a few reservations we continued to see each other again—casually and without any sex for the first few months. (I sometimes thought I was going out with a forty-year-old virgin who had two daughters, and yet there was something magnetizing about her.) As Pat and I look back on those days now, we can both see the half-conscious means we employed to keep each other at an emotional arm's length. Both of us were still hurting from our divorces; neither of us could stand a headlong plunge into intimacy;

memories of what past intimacy had come to were still too strong for that. For my part, I continued to date other women, some of whom I went to bed with. I insisted on my complete independence and refused to make any long-term commitments or promises. I simply had to be free to move at my own speed—and I would have run if Pat had shown even the slightest evidence of possessiveness. Yet I found myself more and more drawn to Pat as we spent evening after evening listening to music, going to restaurants or movies—and talking, talking, talking. Slowly, with one eye constantly cocked on the open door, I was discovering a woman I could be myself with, who in fact would not settle for anything less. I had previously misread and feared her intuitive intelligence, warmth, and aliveness and labeled those qualities "stupid."

In talking over these days later, Pat told me something which I had not known at the time. "I never thought of you as a possible lover at first," she said. "What I saw in you was a friend. I couldn't have taken the intensity of a sexual relationship at the start. I had a lot of anger toward all men. I can remember even being incensed when I thought I saw the supermarket clerk giving me the eye. 'What would your wife say?' was all I could think. You know, all during that time, even though my divorce was final, I kept the fantasy in my mind that my first husband would come back. I had convinced myself that he was sick and that when he got well we would get back together; that was why I still wore my wedding ring when you first met me. I told myself it was too tight to take off. I think that fantasy protected our growing relationship, because it kept me from getting scared off; I could just think of you as a friend. Then I gradually got used to you and found myself missing you when you didn't call. I can remember, when you would leave after a date, having to bite my tongue not to ask when you would call or when I would see you. Part of me knew that you needed that freedom, and I was still caught in my past. But another part of me wanted the completeness of knowing you'd be around. I used to think I was using a typical female ploy—you know, manipulating your man—but now I think I needed the space and time apart as much or more than you did. Any more closeness than we had at that time would have suffocated me.

"You see I was proceeding at my own pace, too—like with the length of time it took me to take off my wedding ring. I can still remember clearly when that happened. It was on a bright and sunny March day, a Tuesday to be exact, three months after we met. I had just finished doing the dishes after eating lunch, and while I was drying my hands with a yellow towel my eyes focused on my wedding ring. As I looked at it I felt it was no longer a part of me. I wasn't married to that man any longer; that ended over a year ago, so why was I still wearing the ring? I finally knew then my marriage had really ended. At that moment it seemed the most natural thing in the world for me to take off the ring I had never taken off in the eighteen years of my marriage. I used a little soap and water and it came off easily. The ring wasn't so tight after all."

TESTING, TESTING, TESTING

However, as we began to make further commitments to each other—Pat through her decision to enter into a closer relationship with me, I through my willingness to acknowledge her importance to me by becoming uninterested in going out with other women—we constantly devised half-conscious ways to test out the strength of our connection with each other. Did we really care for and trust each other? Each of us had "hot buttons" of hurt left over from the past and on occasion one of us would push the other's button. Sometimes we were conscious of what we were doing and could laugh about it; at other times we had raging arguments in which we each unconsciously acted out our fears and asserted the shaky new independent persons we were each becoming.

Peculiar things were happening inside me. Something, I knew not what, was drawing me closer to this woman my head kept claiming I had nothing in common with. Instead of worrying and analyzing this "problem" as I would have done in the past, I surprised myself: I stopped fighting myself and went with the ebb and flow of the relationship—which was becoming increasingly more enjoyable and exciting—trusting the strength of our relationship to arise out of our being together instead of imposing a list of demands as to what we should or shouldn't be with each other. As I look back to that time, I see that I was learning to trust my capacity (which grew stronger as I grew more self-aware) to take creative charge of moving my life in a more satisfying direction, and Pat was doing the same.

I can smile now at some of the "crazy" things I did as we drew closer together, but at the time I was not aware that my actions might have seemed a bit odd. I used to call Pat on a Monday and tell her I'd like to see her Friday—and then would show up unexpectedly at her house on Tuesday. Or I'd say I wouldn't be able to see her the next week, and then would pop in at noon the next day! Pat understood what was happening better than I did at the time. As she later said,

"Your erratic schedule surprised me at first, but then I realized it was your way of saying I'd love to get closer to you but I really must go! You didn't want to be fenced in in any way, because then you would feel trapped. You needed space, just as I did, to get your head straight. I knew you had to do it to heal yourself. So after awhile it seemed normal to me that you were erratic.

"It wasn't just your schedule, either. I could never predict what you'd be like when you came over. You seemed to wear so many different hats. On Monday you'd be happy, feeling you could conquer the world. Tuesday you'd look like a slob, as if the world were on your shoulders. Wednesday you'd be the debonair reporter, grilling and questioning me. Thursday it was the intellectual, still thinking about an article you'd just read—you were in the house with me but really miles away. Friday you'd be all dressed up as if you'd just flown in from the big city. Saturday you were just Mel, warm and loving and open with none of the week's façades. But I loved every one of you. I knew you were trying to find out who you truly were, because I was doing the same thing in my own way."

What I was doing, without consciously knowing it at the time, was testing out my capacity for personal change in my behavior, my ability to relate in new ways in an unprecedented situation. For I was moving into the deep waters of an intimate relationship again, but in a new way, wanting the relationship and at the same time being scared to death of it. "Here is woman who 'seems' to like me as I am," I thought, "but what if that's an act? So I'll do the things that most likely will turn her off and 'prove' I am right in not trusting her. Nothing else seems to turn her off, not even my intellectual snobbism, so why not try new distancing devices to keep me from connecting with her at deep emotional levels?'' Yet there I was with increasing frequency responding to Pat in joyously sexual, sensual, caring, open ways. And I could cry as well as laugh in front of Pat, show my fear and vulnerability (which was particularly strong since I was just starting a chancy new career as a divorce adjustment counselor). Surprise! She accepted it all and helped me transcend my difficulties.

As the relationship grew deeper, I began to believe it was because Pat was changing, but in fact basic changes were occurring within me. I was starting to see her as an individual in her own right and was liking with increasing intensity what I saw: She really was an unaffected woman who had a marvelous capacity to accept people on their own terms.

She had a natural earthiness and a profound love of nature and animals that touched me and sparked me to participate in that love. She had a sense of humor and delighted in her own clowning; we laughed a lot together. She had a quick, native intelligence that could get to the heart of personal problems and cut through intellectual façades. The fact that she had never completed college and was not knowledgeable about intellectual concerns no longer mattered to me. Later, I was to discover she had always had a desire for that knowledge and had wanted to complete college but believed that it was impossible because she was—at forty—too old! Her role as beleaguered housewife, mother of two daughters, as well as part-time jobholder during her marriage had made that desire seem hopeless. (She *did* subsequently return to college two years ago, transforming that impossible dream into a reality.)

I was beginning to feel an aliveness I thought I had lost along with my youth. I'm amazed, as I look back, to recall the enormous release of my energies that our relationship triggered. Where did it come from? Here I was "dating" a woman, staying up till 3 A.M. with her night after night, talking, touching, sharing my hopes and fears—and then arriving at my office at 8 A.M. feeling great. Me, a middle-aged man!

Pat, recalling that time, says she experienced the same sense of renewal. "I had energy I never thought I possessed. All my life I had been an early person, going to bed at ten, getting up at six-thirty. I had to work, too, and get to my job at eight and yet I had energy to spare for seeing and being with Mel after work. The time went by like lightning. Three o'clock in the morning and I would be feeling bright-eyed and bushy-tailed. I used to think everyone had a limited amount of energy that gets used up in the day. Now I know that simply isn't true. If you are turned on to someone or something and feel you are making things in your life better, more energy pours out of you than you ever thought possible."

If, as it has been said, a state of love exists when the welfare of the other person means as much to you as your own well-being, we were getting close to love. Perilously close, and therefore the greater the need for each of us to go to the brink to test our own and each other's commitment to our relationship. It was no accident that the greatest test occurred three days after we had discussed the possibility of renting a house and living together. It started quietly enough. Pat came over for dinner; afterward we watched a discussion on TV of "open" relationships. When it was over, I said I agreed with the speaker who said that monogamy was out of date and that promiscuity in marriage was a perfectly acceptable way of living, provided husband and wife were in agreement. At that Pat exploded. "A lot of phony game-playing" is what she called it. That pushed my panic button. "Look where monogamy has gotten both of us!" I shouted. For three hours we screamed and yelled at each other, Pat arguing for the virtues of monogamy, and I for promiscuity—and each accusing the other of phoniness, deceit, and not really caring. At one in the morning Pat stomped out in a white fury, vowing that it was over, and that she would never, never see me again. I sat alone in the living room, depleted, drained of a rage inside me that had been so excessive to the issue at hand. What the hell had been going on? Why was I advocating the joys of promiscuity as if my life were at stake? It was crazy; the issue was so far removed from my present life as to mean nothing to me. Pat and I had had a strictly monogamous relationship for months and found it totally satisfying. I neither had a need nor a desire to sleep with other women. I was defending an idea I had *once* believed in—and defending it to a point of no return with Pat.

I was trying to sort this out in my mind when she returned forty-five minutes later. Tears were in her eyes, and mine too, as we rushed into each other's arms. For Pat as well as myself, this had been an unknowing test for both of us to find out how firmly we were committed to each other. She later told me just how angry she had been when she left: "You can sleep with every woman in the world if you want to, I thought, but I'll have no part of you. You knew how I felt about that; we'd talked about it before. You knew how angry it made me when you said you regarded having sex with different women as just the same as eating in different restaurants. You knew this was the one issue I simply could not compromise on. I could hardly see to drive home, I was crying so hard, so I pulled off on a side street and really started to weep out my anger. When I was cried out, I began to think with a clearer head, and I could see what you were doing: The same old distancing routine again, but with a different twist. Of course, we were getting so close to each other that the blowup had to happen that evening when things had been going so well between us. The argument had started just after we had a fine dinner, made love, and everything seemed warm and tingly between us. When all this connected in my mind, I knew our relationship hadn't been played out yet. Now that I understood where the pieces of the puzzle fit, it really wasn't a question of who was right or wrong. I knew that your true feelings about monogamy were the ones you were living out in our relationship. Your words were just that, words, a cover-up for the fact that you were falling in love with me, and I with you. When I realized this, I immediately turned around and drove back to your apartment. The question of pride, or of winning or losing the argument, was totally irrelevant.''

That weekend we began looking for a house to rent in which we could live together.

LEARNING, UNLEARNING, RELEARNING

At the time I was experiencing our relationship, I saw it as many things: nurturing, tempestuous, frightening, tender, disturbing, exciting. I really had no idea what would happen, but I was beginning to trust myself enough to allow it to develop of its own momentum—two steps forward, three back; four steps forward, one back. Today I can recognize that the struggle within me was between my past ways of relating and the surfacing trust in my own competence to learn from and improve upon the old ways. The jolt of my divorce had forced me to re-form a number of assumptions I had always accepted without even thinking. I now believed that marriage was not *necessarily* forever; that it was a fact in one's life offering a choice to two people to make it beautiful or ugly, rather than a happily-ever-after solution to all problems. But in my relationship with Pat, I was coming up against other ingrained beliefs. I, like everyone else, had grown up believing that an intimate relationship meant falling in love at first sight, being together all the time, two hearts beating as one, liking only the same things and having only the same friends. Yet my growing love for Pat wasn't following that script. Love at *last* sight, perhaps, but love nonetheless; and none of those other criteria for an intimate relationship were in evidence either. Maybe that old script never was true.

My sense of our growing relationship also reflected my heavier feelings. There was *fear* that the past pain in my life would repeat itself in an eventual parting; *resentment and hostility* at wanting a new, involved relationship with a woman because any other alternative was too painful to consider; *helplessness* as if I were being drawn toward Pat against my will; *despair and depression* in my belief that if the relationship were truly an intimate and loving one it *must* repeat the broken-dreams ending of my past marriage; *anger* at having to give up my lifelong notion that the woman in my life must become solely the extension of all my needs if I were to have a truly satisfying relationship with Pat. And yet . . . things *were* going the way a growing part of me wanted them to go, that part that wanted something better and saw the possibility of achieving it. Often it seemed things were going my way *in spite of myself*, which only meant that I was resisting my growing ability to move beyond the dead end of my past unsatisfying relationships with women because I was afraid of losing my old and familiar "distancing" role. I was letting go of my past notions of what love was all about in the very process of experiencing the good new things that were happening in our relationship. Being in love, I was finding out with Pat, did not demand a strangulation that left out separate quiet times and independent activities for ourselves, nor did it require the sacrifice of my personhood or hers. Those were only unworkable old assumptions, not universal truths. I was learning to relate in new ways that proved those assumptions false, and the fact that I could do so in middle age surprised and delighted me.

The development of our relationship speeded up tremendously when we finally rented a house and moved in together. We were ready for the experience, but not for the implication that it meant eventual marriage. We were still too close to our pasts for that. What is the difference between living together as a monogamous couple and being married? While I cannot speak for those who have never been married before, both Pat and I can say that for us the difference was profound. If we had married then, or agreed that we would marry someday, the relationship would have been burdened with the concepts of marriage each of us had brought from the past. By not being married, we could concentrate on the living together part without the task of living up to the socially defined straitjacketed roles that are so much a part of marriage as we had known it. By so doing, we arrived at our own definition of marriage which accorded with the people we were rather than with the façades society demanded that we hold up. We were not so much breaking a series of past behavior patterns as we were learning our way around what was a new situation for both of us. The process is not dissimilar to a method for improving one's tennis game that W. Timothy Gallway advocates in *The Inner Game of Tennis* (a book that is more about life than about tennis): "We have all had the experience of deciding that we will not hit a tennis ball a certain way again . . . [but] often, in fact, the harder we try to break a habit, the harder it becomes . . . . It is a painful process to right one's way out of a deep mental groove. It's like digging yourself out of a trench. But there is a natural and more childlike method. A child doesn't dig his way out of his old grooves; he simply starts new ones! . . . If you think you are controlled by a bad habit, then you will feel you have to try to break it. A child doesn't have to break the habit of crawling, because he doesn't think he has a habit. He simply leaves it as he finds walking an easier way to get around. Habits are statements about the past and the past is gone."

Learning new habits was not easy for Pat and me. Though we were not married, in many ways our daily lives were like those of a married couple. Time and again we ran into situations reminiscent of the past which triggered off old behavior. Perhaps the most typical recurrence of the past was our inability at first to separate out our needs as individuals from our needs as a couple. Admitting that each of us had differing needs at the same time, which required fulfillment apart from each other, was difficult in the beginning. Initially, we were quick to seek out hurt and rejection, so that when one of us would walk out of a room, distracted or thoughtful, without saying anything to the other person, the one left behind would instantly feel cut off and resentful. I would think, "I didn't do anything, did I? Why should she be leaving me?" and would begin to boil inside. However, a basic trust was growing between us, and in time we learned to stop *assuming* the worst or, if we did feel hurt, to directly discuss what was happening. Both Pat and I learned to say on occasions when we needed time for ourselves, "I'm feeling down or distracted; it's got nothing to do with you—I just need some quiet time for myself right now." Twinges of rejection continued to recur, but we were coming to accept them as memories of the past and not realities of the present. Still, we had to live through such experiences many, many times before we began to feel secure enough in our emotions to feel comfortable in our new ways.

SEPARATING THE PAST FROM THE PRESENT

As we became comfortable in our new ways, the decision to marry emerged as a natural next commitment. Seven months after we had moved in together we set the date. During the months that followed, I remember feeling completely comfortable, even cool, about remarrying, without the slightest sign of uncertainty or fear. But then something happened.

The night before our marriage I was pouring water in a funnel to make some coffee, something I had done innumerable times before without accident. This night, however, I "absentmindedly" missed the funnel and poured the boiling water on my right foot. The slippers I was wearing offered no protection, and instead of immediately putting the kettle back on the stove, I continued to pour the water on my foot until the reality of the pain caused me to deflect the water's direction. "How stupid of me," I yelled in agony. And then I laughed, laughed loud and hard; the laughter seemed inseparable from the pain. I saw the connection immediately, something I could not have done before my relating to Pat: I had just *acted out* all my anxieties and fears about getting married again, which I did not know had been hidden under my cool exterior of the past weeks. The water pouring "mistake" was the way my past ways of relating to women were saying, "You see, you really are a bumbling idiot to believe you can expand your horizons and act differently and more constructively in a relationship. Remember your past— nothing can change for the better! You can't get married tomorrow because you have to go to the hospital and fix your foot instead." But this time there was no doubt within me. My relationship with Pat, *as I had already experienced it*, indeed had proved to be different. The fact that I had already demonstrated that I would relate differently enabled the past (in the form of the accident) to surface up without destroying our relationship. The past was no longer in charge of my new relationship; its power over my forthcoming marriage disappeared in my recognition of this exciting new development within me.

Pat and I married the next day, after I went to the

hospital that night for treatment of a second-degree burn. Instead of a shoe, I sported a bandaged right foot at the ceremony.

Pat and I had traveled more than just three years through a relationship: Each of us had taken what appeared to be a million-mile journey inside ourselves during that time, and arrived at new and more comfortable places inside ourselves. We validated those new places in the words we wrote for our ceremony: ''We come together in marriage to share who we are instead of what we have.''

2 Intimacy Revisited: New Pathways Toward New Relationships

Pat and I have frequently shared the previous chapter with the men and women in our Learning to Love Again groups as a way of helping them reflect on how they can lay the foundations for a lasting love relationship in their own lives. Janet, the woman who wanted to be Number One, said to us after reading it: "It sounds like a happily-ever-after fairy story. Both of you were so very lucky to meet each other. I feel envy, if you must know, because there just aren't any people around that I can experience your kind of relationship with. And that's not because I haven't tried—I've really been out there looking, but I always seem to get burned."

Many of the beginners in a typical LTLA group feel exactly the way Janet did. I remember how puzzled I was when I first heard this reaction. Hadn't I written that our relationship had developed over a three-year period? Hadn't

I indicated that risk, fear, and vulnerability pursued both of us at every stage of our relationship? And wasn't it clear that our relationship had started from scratch and could have ended before it began?

It was Pat who suggested the reason why the real meaning of our story was being overlooked: "Mel, aren't you forgetting that these men and women are stuck in the same place we were at the time we went to that Christmas party? . . . You had just been rejected by a woman you thought you loved, and I was still so scarred that I thought I could never trust enough to be close to a man again. At that time, you and I didn't even know there were new ways in which love could blossom! We were carrying around inside ourselves moldy suitcases stuffed with old attitudes and habits about what love and a good man-woman relationship are all about. We know now that every person who wants to can take the next step in learning to love in new ways, but many persons in their heart of hearts don't believe that's really possible for them. They read our story, then see that their life at the present time is nothing like the way they want it to be.

"It's a healthy sign if they feel envy or anger by passing our story off as a fairy tale. If they didn't react with some hostility toward our story, it would indicate they really are too set in their old ways of looking at their relationships to attempt to try to learn to love in new ways. You see, they want to move ahead and take the next step in a new direction, but don't know where to begin. Since they believe they might fail if they did know, they feel shaky and uncertain. So they protect themselves from these uncomfortable feelings by labeling our story as a form of magic. They think we found a secret formula by sheer luck. What we hope to show is that each and everyone of them has the same possibilities inside himself or herself as we have. They themselves are the secret formula.''

''EASY DOES IT''—OR DOES IT?

The first step in learning to love in a new way is to give up an old and cherished American illusion—the illusion that there is an easy answer to every problem. There are no easy answers or formulas about how you can establish a lasting and satisfying love relationship. For many of you, this may not be the first book you have read on love and personal relationships. If you have found those other books unhelpful, perhaps it's because they made solutions to personal difficulties sound so easy. Catchy phrases, diagrams, and plausible generalizations can give the illusion of helpfulness. If you found that those books didn't help you in your everyday life, there is no need to believe it is your fault and feel you are dense. You see, you were right and those books were wrong. Your own understanding was telling you that there are no easy answers, while the books were telling you easy answers exist. All you can learn from those books is that your situation is hopeless since the advice they give doesn't help you.

I too have been a searcher in the past for the easy answer. However, realistic hope entered my life only when I oh-so-reluctantly—and gradually—gave up the search for nonexistent magic formulas. Consequently, this book you are reading is of a different kind. In it you will discover that new pathways to love indeed exist. You will find the ways in which you will be able to see yourself and others in a more constructive light. In turn, your changed perspective will enable you to initiate and maintain a more satisfying relationship with a special person of the opposite sex than might previously have been possible. The possibility of that happening, however, begins with ending the search for the easy answer, which admittedly isn't easy. Janet had reacted to this statement with a puckish but sad smile: "You mean to say, Mel, that there isn't any Santa Claus?" After I told her, alas, he doesn't exist, Janet paused and thought for a moment. "But can I still believe in the tooth fairy?" she asked hopefully. What Janet will discover is that she herself can become her own Santa Claus and tooth fairy.

YOU ARE A POTENTIAL IN THE PRESENT

When you give up the search for the easy answer you will allow yourself to receive the insight that an improved relationship with the opposite sex originates from a surprising source: Yourself.

I say "surprising" because I have found that most people take it for granted—just as I once did—that they know who they are and therefore can only act in certain ways. So if their relationships with the opposite sex repeatedly end in unsatisfying ways, they can always justify the results by attributing the breakups to external circumstances over which they have no control. As Jerry, a thirty-four-year-old man divorced five years and shoring up the ruins of his sixth shattered affair, philosophized: "I've had a lot of unlucky breaks, I guess. The right woman hasn't come by yet who will see me as I am!"

Perhaps you yourself are at the point in your life where your single-person image seems to be saying the same thing to you as your former married-person image said: Changing your life for the better seems impossible. Carol, an attractive thirty-five-year-old, spotted this tendency in her own current life-style: "I've been divorced five and one-half years and had one fairly long relationship sometime ago that ended badly. I don't like what is happening to me. I find the longer I'm single, the more hardened I seem to get. It's fine to have proven to myself that I'm able to survive on my own and that I'm not the old doormat I once was in my marriage. But the longer I live alone, the more I see I'm getting too self-centered. It's sort of like I'm building a wall around me to protect what I have. This really hit me like a slap in the face two months ago when I spent the night with a man eight years my junior. He never had been married and never had experienced any kind of sharing commitment with anyone. All he cared about was what he wanted both in and out of bed. It was as if I were an object to be used and thrown away when I no longer satisfied his needs. That worried me, because I felt I might be changing into someone like him. How ugly that would be!"

Carol, of course, won't change for the worse, since she is already aware of the dangerous hardening possibility inside herself. Her self-awareness of this negative possibility is a signal-alert that will prevent her from hardening. It will enable her to come to the realization that valuing herself as a single person, being kind to herself and concerned about the quality of the life she is leading, can be her new foundation for reaching out to other people in more fulfilling ways than she has done in the past. Self-esteem is neither selfishness nor irresponsible self-indulgence, which indeed do erect barriers against a close relationship. To the contrary, it is the precondition for developing the capacity to love and be loved in a mature way.

However, the surrounding of oneself with a protective coating of self-centeredness is very common to the not-so-recently divorced. It shows up again and again as a fear of becoming too close to another person, while at the same time desiring that very closeness:

☐ Arnold, forty-seven, divorced eight years ago, has been engaged three times to three different women. He broke his engagement to the first woman three months before the marriage date. The second woman received her termination notice one month before the agreed-upon date. He almost made it to the altar the third time when he ended the relationship two days before the ceremony.

☐ Joan, thirty-six, remarried five years after her divorce. She had lived with Alfred one year before their marriage and saw him during that time in a most favorable light as a "lover." She looked forward with great delight to marrying him. But shortly after the marriage ceremony that delight turned into depression. In her mind, the marriage ceremony and legal piece of paper now meant he was a "husband" rather than a "lover." For Joan, these two qualities were mutually exclusive: No "husband" could also be a "lover." This turned into a self-fulfilling prophecy. One month after the marriage she started divorce proceedings.

☐ Beverly, twenty-nine, was really turned on by Tom, a man she had been seeing three or four times a week over a period of six months. She says it was the best romantic relationship she had experienced in the past three years since her divorce. But Tom recently said to her, "I'm falling in love with you." That was a month ago, and Beverly is finding excuses that somehow prevent her from ever seeing him again.

□   Helene, forty-three, and Jack, forty-two, both divorced seven years ago, are constantly arguing over whether or not their current living-together arrangement is temporary or permanent. Jack says it is temporary and that he is free to leave at any time. Helene insists it is a permanent, committed relationship. Their argument started almost the day they moved in together. They are now in their third year of living together and in their third year of arguing about whether or not the relationship is temporary or permanent. During the past year the argument has escalated to fist-pounding and screaming.

□   Since her divorce six years ago, Joyce, forty-four, re- peatedly falls in and out of love only with married men. She knows beforehand nothing permanent will ever come out of any of these relationships, yet yearns for permanency. "There are no interesting single men around, and, oh, how I wish there were," she keeps on saying.

□   In the last year before Harry's fourteen-year marriage broke up he had no sex with his wife, nor did he have any extracurricular affairs. Since his divorce three years ago at the age of thirty-eight, his sexual experiences with a variety of women have been, according to him, "fantastic." How- ever, in the past three months he has been experiencing bouts of impotence and premature ejaculation, something that nev- er happened before in his life. It all began when Eve, the woman he has been feeling very close to and tender toward, suggested they try living together since they felt so emotion- ally involved and comfortable with each other.

These examples are very similar to the fear-of-closeness-yet-wanting-it that Pat and I experienced. Had I really been so much different from Beverly? She was trying to back away from a love commitment by avoiding Tom, while I had attempted to get out of a similar commitment by scalding my foot the night before my marriage.

I can understand Helene and Jack's trumped-up argument because I had prepared the way to be distanced and rejected by Pat when I created the promiscuity versus monogamy argument. And Pat says, "I can see myself in all of these people in the way I continued to wear my wedding ring after my divorce. I didn't know that ring would distance many men, just as it prevented you from even introducing yourself to me at the party. I felt I was ready to get closer to a man when I saw you at the party. But a part of me was also saying, 'Don't come too near me, I have my wedding ring on.' "

Unless you understand that you may be doing many things to yourself and others to prevent the very thing you want the most from happening, no progress in learning to love again is possible. Remember how in the first few years after your divorce you took personal responsibility to better your own life, and succeeded in doing so by recognizing and ending self-defeating behavior? Once you gained some time and distance living as a single person, you realized that it took two people to create an impossible marriage. Focusing your attention on what went wrong in the way you and your spouse had related in that marriage, rather than on your spouse's actions alone, enabled you to come to terms with your past marriage. It helped you realize that you and your ex-spouse were well-intentioned separate individuals clashing with each other because you were moving in different directions without even knowing it. This enabled you to end the anger and bitterness that could have poisoned your life for years to come. Your energy was then concentrated on living in the present rather than on refighting the long-dead marital battles in your past. In other words, you saw yourself as a potential in the present rather than as a product of your past sour experiences. Consequently, you have become more than you ever thought previously you could become.

Now is the time to apply your hard-earned knowledge that you have the capacity for improving the quality of your life to a new area of need—your need to love and be loved again. In your divorce you embarked on a voyage of self-discovery. That voyage tapped powers within you that you may never have thought you possessed. You had to have intelligence, courage, motivation, openness to new experience, the ability to learn from the past instead of repeating it, in order to move into the new, uncharted waters of single life and survive as effectively as you have. These capabilities haven't died now that you have stabilized your single life. They may be sleeping inside you, but you can awaken them and put them into the service of making a lasting love relationship a reality in your present life.

There is good reason why these capabilities seem to be sleeping so soundly at this time in your life when you need them so urgently. To establish a relationship in which love, friendship, commitment, caring, sharing, companionship, stability, mutual respect, and trust are the end product may require you to again readjust your conception of who you are and what you are capable of becoming. Changing your image of yourself from a married person to a divorced person to a single person of value and worth in your own right is a way station on the road to a fulfilling love relationship. It is, however, a way station you can be stuck at permanently unless you journey into the further reaches of who you are and what you are capable of becoming. The need for love and the giving of love is profoundly a part of what makes us human and originates in one's earliest years. Very young children have been known to waste away and die for the lack of love. To be able to sustain a deep love relationship requires you to expand your knowledge of yourself beyond the knowledge derived from the divorce experience. There is unfinished business in your life apart from marriage and divorce, which subsequent chapters in this book will deal with. Recognizing that unfinished business will enable you to recognize new ways to approach and sustain a meaningful love relationship. To embark on new and more effective ways of relating and loving is to rock the boat of who you think you may be. Of course, you can settle for much less in life by not rocking that boat. Ahead lies the enormous positive reward for which the risk of seeing yourself in a new light will be taken. Behind you lies the familiar, comfortable discomfort of knowing that nothing new will happen in your life and therefore a meaningful love relationship is a hopeless dream. The choice is up to you.

RECOGNIZING HOW YOU LIMIT YOURSELF

Are you currently in a NOBODY-LOVES-OR-CARES-ABOUT-ME mood, or in a WHERE-CAN-I-MEET-THE-RIGHT-PERSON dilemma, or in a RE-JECTED AGAIN situation? If so, the following motto, which I have used in my own life at such times, may prove helpful to you: "Don't just do something, sit there instead."

This motto tells me to stop wallowing in self-pity, or remorse, anger, vulnerability, or bitterness. It says, put those familiar feelings aside for the time being and try to look at your situation from a new perspective. Rather than attributing everything to outside forces over which you claim you have no control, think how you might be setting up the situation to arrive at your dead-end state. Clues to new pathways to a more satisfying love relationship can materialize. But you won't see those clues until you realize that you may be limiting yourself. What you think you can do and what you can do are very different.

I would like to share with you a problem which may show you (just as it did me) how you may be limiting your possibilities for solving dilemmas in your life without being aware that you are doing so. In the figure below, try to connect the nine dots by four straight lines without lifting your pencil from the paper:

You will find the solution on page 49, but before turning to it take as much time as you wish to work out your own solution. If you are like most people, including myself, you will wind up again and again and again with one or more unconnected dots, and with a frustrated feeling that the problem cannot be solved. However, the problem can be solved. Your inability to find the solution has nothing whatsoever to do with incompetence or lack of intelligence, but lies elsewhere. As the presenters of this problem point out:

> Almost everybody who first tries to solve this problem introduces as part of his problem-solving an assumption which makes the solution impossible. The assumption is that the dots compose a square and that the solution must be found within that square, a self-imposed condition which the instructions do not contain. His failure, therefore, does not lie in the impossibility of the task, but in his attempted solution. Having now created the problem, it does not matter in the least which combination of four lines he now tries, and in what order; he always finishes with at least one unconnected dot . . . [and] will never solve the task.*

If you make the *one* unwarranted assumption that the nine dots compose a square, which prevents you from solving the problem, imagine the *torrent* of unwarranted assumptions you may be making about what intimacy and a lasting

---

*Paul Walzlawick, John Weakland, and Richard Fisch, *Change: Principles of Problem Formation and Problem Resolution*. New York: W. W. Norton & Co., 1974, p. 25.

love relationship consist of and how you go about attaining them!

When we met, Pat and I were burdened by many unwarranted assumptions. And if we had not become aware of them and substituted new realities for outmoded, unexamined beliefs, our relationship would have ended before it began. The assumptions that weighed us down are the same as those many of the beginners in our LTLA Seminars are confronting for the first time in their lives. While you examine these assumptions, which are listed below, think about whether or not you too may be locking yourself into a room labeled "dead end" and throwing away the key:

Do you assume that love means being strangled or devoured by the person you love?

I've heard those phrases used many times, frequently out of my own mouth in the past. Everyone experiencing difficulties in establishing a close relationship I mentioned earlier in this chapter felt this way. They all passionately want the salt that makes life worth living, which can only be attained through a meaningful love relationship—the salt of companionship, stability, feedback, caring, trust, and the glowing sex that is the product of commitment. But all of them feel the price for these valuables is too high for them to pay. Put-downs, jealousy, rejection, denial of their own needs, and eventual boredom are the inevitable penalties they feel they "must" pay as the price of commitment. After all, that's what happened in their past marriages and subsequent relationships, they keep saying. So their response is to back away from a close commitment even though their souls are crying out for it!

"Getting hooked again? No way!" says Jess, a thirty-four-year-old man divorced three years ago. "My ex-wife, Harriet, was a great teacher—she taught me women are ballcrushers. I never, never won an argument in all the years we were married. The day I left I told her, 'Dammit, Harriet, you're always right even when you're wrong!' Sure, I would love to meet someone different now, but what's to show that any of them are different from Harriet or that I would act any different?"

If you feel this way, reflect on the reality that you are a potential in the present, not a victim of your past. You have already experienced that fact by what you have done with your life since your divorce. If you were like most of us, you had assumed marriage was forever and that surviving on your own was inconceivable. You have already proved to yourself that you can relate to the challenge of being single in new ways. Why then limit your possibility for happiness by assuming you can't relate to the challenge of a lasting love relationship in new ways.

Do you assume that meeting that special person who you will love and who will return that love is a matter of luck?

I had lived with this assumption until I met Pat. It was a marvelous cop-out for me, since I did not have to take any responsibility for creating the conditions in which I would be able to take advantage of luck should it arise. Frequently, in the past, I closed out the chance for luck to materialize by turning down social engagements because I assumed that everyone present would be dull or "losers." How could I ever be "lucky" if I ran away from places where luck was likely to show itself? Of course, an element of luck enters into meeting a special person, but you have more power to

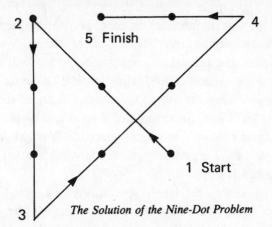

The Solution of the Nine-Dot Problem

create luck than you think. I am reminded of Paula, fifty-two, a woman who attended one of my seminars four years after her divorce,who used to complain about how unlucky she was in not finding a man she could be committed to. In a recent letter to me she said: "You can probably tell I am now enjoying my life—my job, my painting, my friends. Best of all, I've stopped believing I'm unlucky. As my friend Alice remarked to me at a party four months ago, 'Paula, people are out there looking for you!' I liked that thought, and since then I've been going to places where new friends or maybe a new lover can find me. There are now three new men in my life that I can call friends. And one of those relationships is becoming more than friendship."

Do you assume that adult love is the same as adolescent love?
My own experience tells me that people do not necessarily grow wiser in understanding what love is all about just because they grow older. The many men and women in their twenties, thirties, forties, and fifties relating their stories of

current breakups and disillusionments often sound like teen-agers. Adolescent fantasies die hard, particularly the notion of Instant Romantic Love. The adolescent confuses love with infatuation, the immediate, overwhelming physical attrac-tion and the excitement of feeling ten feet tall in the loved one's eyes. Then the inevitable adolescent disenchantment occurs. Sir Walter Scott summed it up almost two hundred years ago in words that sound modern: "What we love in these early days is generally rather a fanciful creation of our own than a reality."

The adolescent labels sex, thrills, and good times "love." And when these diminish in intensity, he or she identifies the loss of excitement as the end of love and the time to seek a new partner to recharge the sexual-sensual batteries. His or her partner may change, but the unexamined assumption that Instant Romance is the definition of love is carried over into each new affair.

To love, either as an adolescent or an adult, is to indeed experience the delights of a sexual-sensual turn-on. Such physical attraction is the precondition for all love relation-ships. However, the adolescent believes that the turn-on is love, rather than a starting point for its satisfactory develop-ment. How many of us, now that our own adolescence has long since past, are still buying that adolescent fantasy? Nick, a forty-three-year-old man divorced five years ago, speaks for many of these men and women I have encoun-tered: "I find my relationship with women I'm attracted to changing every three months," he told me. "The relation-ship is always something different than it was when it started, and it always ends in a split-up. Like it's a one-month honeymoon, a one-month marriage, and one-month later a divorce. It's like a soap opera with a beginning, a middle, and an end. At the start it's very tempestuous and there are tremendous highs and tremendous attraction. Then we kind of look at each other's flaws a little bit. And in the last month the flaws are great big gaping holes, so that we can't stay in the relationship. I checked around and found out a lot of other divorced men and women I know have had the same kind of experience. Maybe God didn't intend us to have any love relationship last longer than three months.''

A more accurate way of putting it might be that God didn't intend us to remain adolescents forever. In a lasting adult love relationship, love shows many aspects besides the erotic one. There is also the love that cares about and respects the partner as a person in his or her own right, with flaws included; the love that gives as well as receives; the love that offers feedback and understanding; the love that is a constant and trustworthy commitment even when the conflicting needs of each of the lovers may edge their relationship near the breaking point. And there is the self-love that is the soil in which these other kinds of love flourish, as Anaïs Nin points out: ''How could we love, how could we give, how could we trust, how could we share what we didn't have to give? If we did not spend some time creating ourselves in depth and power, with what were we going to relate to others?''

Do you assume that you can be attracted to only one type of person?
   If you are repeatedly going out with, sleeping with, or living with one type of person and the relationship always ends unsatisfactorily, then you've bought this assumption even if you deny it intellectually. Certainly I had, before I met Pat. By doing so I had denied myself the opportunity to experience new kinds of attraction that might prove

more satisfying to me than the old kind. I had seen myself as the kind of guy who could be interested only in women who were college graduates and knowledgeable about literature and the arts in the same way I was. I had felt I could be accepted by women only because of my book-learned intelligence. Therefore, I would hide the rest of me, since I felt that any woman I thought attractive would not like my other aspects. So I gravitated, without being aware of it, to women who reflected only the intellectual part of me.

However, I was ready to be receptive to a new type of attraction from a new type of woman when I met Pat. (I was a slow learner, but I eventually had come to see the truth of W. C. Field's statement: "If at first you don't succeed, try, try, again; then quit—there's no use being a damn fool about it.) Nobody was more surprised than I was when I found I was becoming attracted to a person I had previously believed was not my style. My growing relationship with Pat enabled me to see that the undeveloped parts of myself (my humor, my love of nature, my spontaneity, my unsuspected emotional range) could flourish in the new environment of a woman whose personality expanded my own sense of myself.

Pat says we were mirror images at the time we met: "I too felt ready for a new type of attraction when you entered the room at that party. I could show my intelligence to you without being put down for it. I could be just me without any pretense. At long last I could expose the earthy woman in me that I had hidden under the cute little girl façade I presented to everyone in so many years of my adult life."

Ted, a forty-nine-year-old man who remarried five years ago after being divorced six years, explained in his own way something similar to what I had experienced with Pat. "If anyone had told me I would ever marry a person like Lee before I met her, I would have called him crazy," says Ted. "Lee is my age, and is on the short, dumpy side, and works as an insurance secretary. I always thought I was the kind of guy who only went for younger women on the tall, slim side and that I would never want a working wife. But Lee is so beautiful, really. She has a fun personality and a lively smile and is as bright as a new penny. She's warm and tender and cares about me. When we make love, the way she responds makes me feel she's the most beautiful woman in the world. And since she enjoys her work, she is a happy woman, not the grouch my ex-wife was. I still get kidded by some of my friends who like to remind me now and then about my former taste in women. But I just smile—they don't know what they are missing!"

Why not let yourself be receptive to new types of attraction? To try it may mean finding out you may like it.

Do you assume that you know how to accurately assess the progress of an adult love relationship that might prove to be satisfying and lasting?

Perhaps you cut your losses too soon, not giving relationships the space and time to blossom. Or you misinterpret motives and make snap judgments about people you might like to know better, and then it's too late. If so, you join the ranks of millions of other men and women who have done and are doing exactly these things.

There is Edie, for example, who says she will never go out with the same man twice if he doesn't "prove" that he is an interesting and fun person on the first date. And there is

Jason, who cuts women out of his life if he doesn't make out the night of the first date. Then there are the many men and women like Russell and Iris who see a slight resemblance to their ex-spouse in the eyes, mouth, hair, or smile of the person they meet and instantly dislike that person because of the superficial similarity.

I know that it's not out of a lack of intelligence or insight that potentially satisfying relationships are killed off before they begin to live. It is usually because most people have never learned that an adult love relationship, a meaningful relationship, is a process over time. Adult love is the freely given gift of their whole personalities that two people shower on each other because that gift mutually enhances their lives. A gift of such enormous value cannot be expected to materialize immediately, since adult love is not a reward for two weeks' or a month's good behavior. Your whole sense of who you are and what you might become is at stake. It takes time for two people to expose the widest range of who they are to each other and confirm that they like what they see. Then, and only then, are you in a position to determine whether or not that relationship might harbor the potential of developing into a lasting one. It took three years of relating for Pat and me to reach the point of taking the risk of closely committing ourselves to each other by remarrying. That is not an exceptional period of time for not-so-recently divorced people. You as the unique individual you are will develop your own internal sense of what is the appropriate time in your life to begin to live a relationship in the new way.

In the above paragraph I indicated that Pat and I "took the risk" of a close commitment. The risk, which we have found enormously well worth the taking, is that a lasting relationship can only be a relationship worthy of lasting, and it cannot be guaranteed in advance to last for any specified period of time. It must allow for the space for two people to grow together and grow separately, otherwise it will self-destruct. The fact that you may not have such a relationship now doesn't mean you can't or won't have it. All it means is that you have learned from society, from family life in the past, from TV and movie fantasies, the ways in which an adult love relationship can shrivel rather than grow. I had to reach my middle years before I realized that I had been programmed by such external forces to defeat my own best interests. My attitude about my becoming aware that there are new pathways to love rather late in life is: Isn't it great that I found out now rather than ten years from now, or never! Since each of us can grow in self-awareness and improve our lives at any age, there is no real reason for hopelessness or despair.

The following guidelines, based on Pat's and my story in the preceding chapter, can help clarify the growth process of an adult love relationship:

1. Focus your attention, intelligence, sensitivity, and energies on the adult possibilities that are available to you in the present instead of reliving the adolescent fantasies of the past. If you have learned to approach a relationship the wrong way, you can also learn to approach it the right way.

2. Approach a new relationship as an adventure in mutual discovery which takes time to unfold. First impressions are frequently misleading.

3. Your sense of self-worth will determine the kind of

person you attract. You do the attracting as much as the other person. To a very great extent, the possibilities of developing a love relationship are determined by the qualities you exhibit in the relationship. If you show little of your total personality, expect little in return.

4. Tear up any hidden checklist your mind may be compiling for what THE RIGHT GUY or THE RIGHT WOMAN for you must be like. When that ''right'' person actually arrives, he or she may be surprisingly and delightfully different from your original imaginings.

5. Discard any preconceived timetable if you wish a meaningful relationship to develop. The surest guarantee that a relationship will toboggan to the depths is to demand in advance that it ''should'' ascend in a prescribed period of time to ecstatic heights.

6. Permit yourself to live in the relationship rather than just visit in it. If you back away from a relationship when problems arise, you are denying yourself the opportunity to make that relationship a more meaningful one. Dealing openly and constructively with the difficulties of developing mutual trust and respect can only deepen a relationship that holds promise. To demand only sweetness and light in a relationship is to deny yourself the possibility of any lasting adult love connection.

7. Since you and the person you are relating to are separate and unique individuals, recognize that the person is proceeding at his or her own pace, just as

you are doing. That pace may not be the pace you are moving at, but should be acknowledged and respected and allowed for without judgment. You would resent being pressured to love on demand— and so would the other person.

8. If you experience uncertainty, anxiety, and vulnerability, recognize that they are the normal signs that a meaningful relationship may be developing. To learn to love in new ways means letting go of old ways of relating. Until you are comfortable in your new ways you are bound to feel uneasy. Consequently, these "negative" feelings may be the very signs that something profoundly "positive" is happening in the relationship.

I have reserved for the conclusion of this chapter an assumption that, more than any other, causes breakups of relationships that might have developed into something satisfying and lasting:

Do you assume that you know what another person is like on the basis of a single party acquaintanceship or dinner date? Or even before you meet that person?

An interesting discussion centered around this issue in a recent LTLA Seminar:

Janice, an attractive woman in her mid-thirties and divorced for five years, said she had been out only twice in the past year and both instances involved only one-time, nonsexual dinner dates. One of the men was an engineer, the other an accountant. "I should have known better," she sighed. "All accountants are boring and engineers are just as bad, so restricted in their interests. Now before I go out with a man, I first have to know what he does for a living.''

Upon hearing this, Ken, a man of the same age, asked, ''What do you think I do for a living?'' Janice guessed he was a musician, because he seemed so spontaneous and warm. ''No, Janice,'' Ken replied, ''I'm an engineer, but I am also a man who paints; I volunteer at a mental health center; I love kids and have a passion for sailing.'' This exchange caused Jim, a quiet, bookish man in his forties who is an army electronics expert, to comment, ''I always hide the fact that I'm in the army when I go out on a first date. It's only after there's something going between us that I tell her I'm an army man. Otherwise, it blows the evening from the start. The woman gets suspicious and distant. I can almost see the wheels inside her head turning: 'An army man out for a one-night lay. Coarse and insensitive.' It's really very discouraging.''

Sally, a petite woman in her late twenties, then said: ''The wrong assumption about what a word might mean can also break up something that might have been nice. Like the word 'fragile' for example. Three months ago I went out with a man, Roger, who seemed attractive and fun. But at the restaurant we went to for dinner he said I looked so fragile. Something inside me turned into ice when I heard that word. I assumed he was insulting me. I'm strong, not fragile. I walked out on my violent husband three years ago and am able to survive alone even though he has given me a lot of hassles and threats. That proves I'm not fragile. Roger so turned me off by calling me fragile that I never went out with him again. But I saw him by chance at a party last week. I simply had to go over and talk with him to find out why he said I was so fragile, because that word really needled me. Well, imagine my surprise when he told he had meant it as a compliment, not a put-down. I felt so embarrassed, because he said that to him 'fragile' meant I had a delicate type of beauty!''

Emily, a forty-one-year-old woman in her sixth year of divorce, was thoughtfully listening to this discussion. When it ended, she said, ''I've learned the hard way in my life that 'assume' is really three words in one. These words are 'ass,' 'you' and 'me.' I have come to realize that to assume I know what you as a person are thinking and feeling and doing in your life—without even asking you or bothering to find out where you are really at—can only make an *ass* out of *me* in regard to *you*!''

3 "Yes, But..."

"Yes, but where do I begin?" you may be asking by this time. If you are in any way like most of the not-so-recently divorced men and women in my Learning to Love Again Seminars, you may be saying what they initially say:

□　"Yes, BUT I've already tried everything—singles bars, church dances, social clubs, school courses, private parties. You name it, I've done it and it's a downer every time."

□　"Yes, BUT where are all the interesting men? They're either married or in hiding. The only men around are other women's rejects."

□　"Yes, BUT where are all the interesting women? They're either too pushy or too silent. All they give me is a dose of instant impotency."

□　"Yes, BUT where can I meet somebody nice? It's all so degrading, the body shops, the singles groups, the personal column ads. So instead of going out any more, I've become a TV junkie.''

□   "Yes, BUT everyone I meet is a loser. All the divorced guys are broke or want to get into my pants five seconds after we meet. And all the rest just want to do my hair.''

□   "Yes, BUT where can I find an interesting woman I can talk to that's attractive? It's very easy to get laid, but then I wake up wondering who is this lump of flesh beside me and why did I bother?''

□   "Yes, BUT let's face it, most women over thirty-five are wrecks with flabby thighs, scrawny necks, and tits down to their belly button. The classy lookers are all taken.''

□   "Yes, BUT every man I meet in his forties, which is my age, wears a rug, has a potbelly and a personality like flat soda water.''

□   "Yes, BUT what if I make another mistake? Whenever I think about going out with another woman, I feel like I'm standing on a corner waiting for one of my mistakes to walk by and claim me.''

□   "Yes, BUT people are so blind. I'm a sensitive, warm, fun-loving person, so why do they overlook me every place I go?''

□   "Yes, BUT every man discriminates against a woman my age. As soon as I tell a man I'm forty, it's a turn-off.''

□   "Yes, BUT I've even tried the computer dating services, and a lemon turns up every time.''

□   "Yes, BUT I work and have two young children to take care of, so it's impossible for me to get out of the house and meet people.''

□   "Yes, BUT men don't like women who have their children living with them like I have, so where does that leave me?''

□ "Yes, BUT all the women I meet only want shallow relationships. They say I come on too close, too fast and then they back away from me."

□ "Yes, BUT I seem to fall into short-term relationships with women all the time. It always happens that they want to get their hooks into me."

□ "Yes, BUT men want only the young chicks. I feel like I'm over-the-hill at thirty."

□ "Yes, BUT the only people I meet are manipulative game players. How can I ever trust anyone again?"

These complaints must be taken seriously. The men and women who voice them are hurting. These people are very much concerned about the quality of their current relationships—or lack of relationships—with the opposite sex. Many of them have tried earnestly and repeatedly to improve their situation. They have met, or attempted to meet, new people, only to find themselves for the ninety-ninth time back where they started from. Hoping for something better, many will try again today or tomorrow or the next weekend. They quite rightly refuse to settle for less; yet somehow they know before they go out again that the next time they try will be no different from the last time.

So where, then, to begin?

BEGIN AT THE BEGINNING

If you are feeling this way and Yes-Buts are running through your mind, the time has come to look at your situation in a *new* way. The beginning point is the situation you find yourself in right now: Instead of repeating your same activities of going out or not going out, of digging your worry-trench deeper and deeper, STOP! Give yourself some quiet time to reflect and reexamine what you are doing and why your activities seem to get you nowhere. Look at your situation as if it were a stranger rather than an old friend and you will then notice what your Yes-Buts have in common with each other:

1. All Yes-Buts assume you are in a situation you can't control. You feel you are an effect, not a cause.

2. All Yes-Buts are judge-jury-and-executioner statements, and you play all three roles. The culprit must be sought out, blamed, and condemned for creating your discomfort.

3. All Yes-Buts assume the inevitability of failure should you once again attempt to establish a lasting love relationship. Even if you say "Yes, but I'm afraid of making another mistake," you assume making a "mistake" is a malign fate that is dogging your steps.

4. All Yes-Buts assume that you have done all you possibly can to improve your chances for a lasting love relationship.

Are the four assumptions listed above true or false? If they are true, then all you can do is cut your losses and settle for less in life than you really hope for. If they are false, then what can you do to improve your situation that you haven't already tried, since you believe you've tried everything? Either way seems like a dead end.

However, this blind alley has an open door when you realize that these four assumptions are at the same time *both* true and false, depending on what reality you are paying attention to. Every person on this earth lives in *two* realities, rather than one:

1. There is the reality *outside* yourself, which is the reality of the world around you. This reality presents *factual* truths that are present in the world regardless of how you feel about them. Divorce, marriage, death, taxes, are examples of factual truths.

2. There is the equally important reality *inside* yourself, which is the reality of what you are currently feeling. The truths this reality presents to you are *emotional truths* that exist inside yourself. If, right now, you are feeling hopeless or bitter or frustrated or sad about the possibility of attaining a lasting love relationship, you are experiencing an emotional truth about yourself. The experience is real to you, and therefore it is true.

All too often all of us mistake the reality of the world inside us for the reality of the world outside. *What may very well be true for what is happening inside of us may very well be false for what is happening in the world around us.* In separating these two realities in your own life, you can see how the four assumptions listed above can be both true and false for you:

1. Your feelings of frustration and failure are emotional truths. Your conviction that you have no other choice but to repeat your old attempts to improve your situation is the reality of the world *inside* yourself.

2. But the world *outside* yourself is far wider and has many more choices than you may be aware of. In this sense, the way in which you are presently seeing your situation is *factually* false.

For example, the factual truth of the world outside

yourself reveals that each year over a million men and women meet each other and remarry; that many people meet new, nice, interesting people anywhere and everywhere, including bars and singles clubs, and begin relationships that last; that many women do find attractive, interesting men just like men find such women; that many women with children meet men who like children; that many men and women find age irrelevant and establish lasting love relationships even though there is a decade or two difference between them; that many women with young children are not housebound and find ways of going out and meeting people; that many men and women have met people in their own age bracket—and will meet new ones in the future—who turn them on.

Are you so very different from these men and women? Not in the least. It is not because you or other people you meet are less attractive or less available that you find yourself at a dead end. Instead, it is the way you see and understand yourself in your present situation that is creating the blind alley you feel yourself in. This statement should not surprise you, since you already learned the truth of it in your creative divorce experience. Now is the time to apply that hard-earned knowledge to this new stage in your life, the stage in which you want a lasting love relationship in addition to your having a secure single-person identity.

YOUR ELEVEN LIFELINES TO LEARNING TO LOVE AGAIN

Your Yes-Buts have been blinding you to the fact that you have already laid the foundation inside yourself to improve the quality of your relationships with the opposite sex.

The lessons you learned from your divorce experience were strong and valuable lessons. They were forged in the furnace of a major crisis in your life and as such served as your lifelines to a better future. *They can be applied by you with positive effect to any new impasse in your life, since your personal growth didn't end when your divorce experience ended.* Learning to love again is the challenge of a new stage in your personal growth, just as making your divorce a creative experience was the challenge of your previous stage. Responding effectively to this new challenge to create new and more fulfilling love relationships requires tapping the knowledge you have already learned from your divorce experience. That knowledge consists of what I call "Your Eleven Lifelines to Learning to Love Again." I'm sure you will recognize them as you read the listing below:

1. The way you saw yourself after your divorce determined how you dealt with it. When you saw yourself as a guilt-ridden failure, your actions confirmed that failure over and over again. But when you subsequently saw yourself as an intelligent, well-intentioned human being, fallible like everyone else, who was capable of learning from the past rather than repeating it, positive things began to happen in your freshly-singled life.

2. The way you understood and reacted to the world outside yourself determined whether or not you limited or expanded your opportunities to improve the quality of your life as a divorced person. When you felt the entire outside world was condemning or rejecting you, you wallowed in self-pity and

blamed others for your situation. But when you realized that this attitude was a millstone you were placing around your own neck, positive things in your life became possible again: There were new people out there who liked you, and there were new organizations that offered you the emotional support that helped you extend your horizons.

3. You found you could surprise yourself. You had the capacities and resources to survive as a single person, even though you thought at first you had none. Even more important, you found out that you could relate in new and better ways to your children, to friends, to relatives, to strangers.

4. Regardless of your age, you discovered you could grow and change for the better or could embark on new projects and gain skills you never thought possible before your divorce.

5. You learned to re-examine the values you had lived by and discarded those you found wanting. You discovered that life is an affair of people rather than things, that what is most valuable in life is how you relate to others and how they relate to you. More open and empathic relations with your children, for example, proved more important than a new television set or a new car had been in your married life.

6. You learned that nothing positive in your post-divorce life could happen unless you yourself made the effort to make it happen. You had to examine the ways you might be defeating your best interests, and then act in new ways. If you were

nonassertive, you became more assertive; if you had no business skills, you took courses; if you were lonely, you called up people without waiting to be called by them. In the process of doing so, you found out that your greatest fear was fear itself. Doing something new was far less scary than you imagined.

7. You learned to respect the uniqueness of each person. You found out you were a unique person in your own right and that your children and your ex-spouse also were separate individuals rather than extensions of your needs. Your ex-spouse was not the "monster" you thought he or she was once you began to realize that "differentness" was not the same as "badness." Differences in personality were to be acknowledged, understood, and dealt with rather than to be labeled bad or evil.

8. You learned not to make flip judgments about other people. Just as you found you had a wider range of emotions, interests, and abilities than you had ever suspected, you found that your children were more perceptive than you had ever realized (Didn't they tell you they knew your divorce was imminent long before you realized it?). Many of you discovered your parents to be more knowledgeable and caring than you gave them credit for. They had known about the irreconcilable differences between you and your ex-spouse years before your divorce; and they were more compassionate and understanding than you ever thought possible.

9. You learned there was a readiness time for coping with your problems. All problems couldn't be solved at once. Taking one day at a time and solving the problems that day enabled you to solve other problems as they arose. The little things you did that demonstrated you could survive on your own were stepping-stones to solving larger problems. (Remember when you thought you could never handle the household repairs now that your husband was no longer around? Remember when you felt you would starve to death or be drowned in your pile of dirty clothes now that your wife no longer supplied household services?)

10. You learned to separate the past from the present and began to live in the present. Instead of worrying over past mistakes or obsessing over nostalgic remembrances, you learned to recognize the newness in each new day. You began to deal with things as they are rather than as they used to be or should be.

11. You learned to separate what society programmed you to believe you were from what you yourself wanted to be at this time in your life. You then acted constructively on what you wanted for yourself. This was best expressed by Peggy, a thirty-four-year-old woman who told me, "When I was a little girl, I was somebody's daughter. . . . When I was a teen-ager, I was somebody's girl friend. . . . Then I became somebody's wife. . . . Now that I'm divorced, I'm somebody!"

RECONNECTING WITH YOUR INNER RESOURCES

Why do we forget these eleven hard-earned lessons of past experience? Like so many others, I forgot them in the early stages of my own learning to love again period. Part of the answer lies in our yearning for stability to enter our lives again after contending with the crisis uproar of our divorce. Stability, peace, and predictability mean more in our new single life than they might have meant before. The rituals and reactions we have created for ourselves in building our secure single-person identities are highly valued. We treasure the freedom to do things because they suit us, rather than because they suit others. As one woman, speaking for so many of us, said, "I don't 'should' on myself any more!"

Consequently, we compartmentalize ourselves and concentrate on reconstructing our lives on a single-person basis. A part of us doesn't want to change again. "Hold fast to what we have, it's liable to be taken away" is the unspoken warning in our feelings.

We put to use the eleven lifelines during the earlier stages of our divorce when we were changing and growing and meeting effectively the new challenge of daily life. But a price had to be paid for attaining our new goal of establishing a secure single-person identity inside ourselves. That price was the disruption of our self-defeating old habits and taken-for-granted ideas about ourselves. Positive change can seem at first as scary as change for the worse, since it involves taking risks and becoming vulnerable again. But once we started to discover the wider range of who we are and what new things we could do for ourselves, we were rewarded for the risks we took with a newfound sense of personal security and stability. However, when our need for a new, lasting love relationship begins to emerge, it creates difficulties as well as possibilities. We feel threatened by the need while we want its fulfillment. To share our life with another person means to lose our single-person freedom and the stability of our new life-style. We remember our pain, vulnerability, and the disruption of our image of ourselves when our precious, close commitment ended in divorce. Our feelings are mixed: part of us wants to distance ourselves from the new people in order to protect ourselves from reliving the remembered pain of the past, while another part of us wants to move closer, provided we are guaranteed happiness.

If you are a "Yes-Butter," recognize that your mixed feelings may be the reason for the dead-end situation you find yourself in. Acknowledging your mixed feelings is the precondition for learning to love again in new, more fulfilling ways. What you may be saying and what you may be doing could be two very different, and self-defeating, things. The part of you that wants a lasting love relationship may make you say: "Oh, how I wish I could find a person I could share my life with!" But your actions could be saying, "Don't come too close to me, even if you love me and I love you; I don't want to be hurt again."

Alan, a thirty-seven-year-old, lively, intelligent, electronics technician who had attended a Learning to Love Again Seminar last year, vividly exemplified this push-pull way of talking and acting. Throughout most of the ten sessions of the seminar he was the most vocal asserter of his determined desire to find a woman he could share his life with. "But no matter how hard I try," he kept saying, "I can't meet anyone that appeals to me even though I've been divorced for four years. And, boy do I try! I'm not a stay-at-home kind of guy."

Six months later a changed Alan called me up: "I had to tell you, Mel, what I learned about myself. Maybe it can help others like me. Just after the seminar ended I met Lisa, a great person, and we're seeing a lot of each other. We're very straight and open with each other, so when I told her how lucky it was that we got together, she said luck had nothing to do with it. Would you believe it, she said I spent most of my efforts avoiding her rather than trying to know her better! That surprised me, because I was very much attracted to her from the first time we met at a mutual friend's party, and I thought I had showed I was."

I asked Alan if he and Lisa would share their experience with me at my office, and they subsequently did so. Here is what Lisa said:

"When we first met we exchanged phone numbers and Alan gave me every indication he would call me soon. I was really attracted to him and hoped he would ask me out. So what happened? Nothing for three weeks. I then decided to call him first and we had a great dinner date. The next time he did the calling and asked me out for Saturday night. I told him I was tied up that night, which was true, but that I'd love to go out with him the next Saturday. His response surprised me. He was silent for what seemed like ages. Then he said, sort of hurt-like, "Well I don't know. I can't plan my life that far in advance."

After that phone call I didn't hear from him. Nothing but silence. I began to think he was rejecting me, but that idea didn't seem to make sense since we had had such a marvelous time together on the first dinner date and he had told me how much he liked me. So, again I took the initiative and called him three days before the Saturday night that I had suggested we go out. That took some doing on my part since I took the risk of being rejected by him. But I long ago learned that nothing ventured is nothing gained, and that sometimes you get rejected but more often you are pleasantly surprised. Rejection isn't really that painful—who can be liked by everyone? You know what? He sounded so happy to hear from me and said of course he would go out with me that Saturday night. That was the turning point in our relationship and it's been fine ever since. If I had been my old self of five years ago, our relationship would have ended before it started. But I've learned to be assertive and recognize that what many people say and what they do are often two very different things. It is like they are sending out double signals. I've found out it is better to stay with such a situation if I'm attracted to a person and finally get a straight signal rather than play coy or run away."

Alan had listened intently to Lisa's statement and then shared his point of view:

"Everything Lisa said is true. I wanted so very much to know her better from the first time I met her. But I was afraid she would reject me. Sure she gave me her phone number, but I thought that might be only out of politeness to my request for it. I started to call her a dozen times before she actually called me for that first date. I got the sweats every time I picked up the phone because I thought—'What if she turns me down?' Was I happy when she called! I admit I was disappointed when Lisa couldn't go out with me on the

Saturday night I suggested. I thought she was rejecting me by putting me off a week. I didn't want her to get the idea that I wasn't booked up in advance like she was, so I played it cool. . . ." At that point Lisa laughed. "Yes," she said, "you played it so cool you almost froze me out of your life!"

IDENTIFYING THE PAST IN YOUR PRESENT BEHAVIOR

The hope that a special person or persons will acknowledge and treasure us as uniquely valuable persons is deeply rooted. We learn the ways in which to be lovable and loved in the earliest years of our lives. Before you and I were six years old, we learned from our mothers and fathers what it means to love and be loved.

Dr. John Bowlby, the noted authority on how children learn to love, has this to say on this subject:

No variables, it is held, have more far-reaching effects on personality development than have a child's experiences with his family: for, starting during his first months in his relationship with his mother figure, and extending through the years of childhood and in adolescence in his relations with both parents he builds up working models of how attachment figures are likely to behave towards him in any of a variety of situations; and on those models are based all his expectations, and therefore all his plans, for the rest of his life. . . . An unwanted child is likely, not only to feel unwanted by his parents, but to believe that he is essentially unwantable, namely—unwanted by anyone. Conversely, a much loved child may grow up to be not only confident of his parents' affection but confident that everyone else will find him lovable too. . . .*

Most of us grew up being loved in certain ways, yet never felt the love we got was enough, or the kind we really needed. We had to prove ourself lovable by acting like our parents wanted us to. We learned that love was a reward and punishment system; we were loved for what we did, not for what we were.

All too often we may be projecting our past habits of loving into present situations without knowing we are doing so. That very unawareness can prevent us from taking advantage of today's real choices and possibilities.

When I was a sales manager years back for a reducing company, I saw many very attractive but anxious women in their early thirties. Most of these women had reached a dead end in their marriages. Their husbands were unattentive, bored, or having affairs. The women believed the only way their marriages could be "saved" was by recapturing the figures they had had when they were twenty. "If my hips were not so large, or my stomach more firm, John would still love me" was the way they viewed their situation. Thick hips, sagging breasts, flabby thighs, eye wrinkles, or being five pounds heavier than they were ten years ago were the problem as they saw it. If they firmed their bodies, family difficulties would vanish, they would again be lovable and loved.

They usually succeeded in improving their physical

---

*John Bowlby, *Separation*. New York: Basic Books, 1973, pp. 204-205, 369.

condition, but their marriages continued to deteriorate. Some of them were shocked and puzzled to find out later that the women their husbands were having affairs with were dowdier and heavier than they were.

These people are what I call *The Externalizers*. They grew up believing that everything could be solved by a new dress or a new hairdo. And when the dress or the hairdo no longer worked, they despaired. The idea that there was more to love than appearance never entered their minds, since they had grown up believing that their parents loved them mostly because of the way they looked. These women lacked any sense of self-esteem since they defined their value, and the value of others, by appearance, money, and status. They put their energies toward accumulating things rather than relating to people.

When new possibilities for love enter our life, we may be denying their existence if we continue to define our own lovability and capacity to love on the basis of how we learned to love in our earliest years. Getting in touch with the truths of that past and acknowledging the reality of their existence and their possible interference in our present life is the push we need to move us beyond the Yes-But stage.

How did you learn to love? Do you recognize something of yourself in the following personality types that appear so frequently in my Learning to Love Again groups?

□   *The Don't-Make-Wavers* are the people whose experiences taught them that love means the absence of punishment. Mom and Dad never listened to them or respected their point of view. Remaining unassertive, inconspicuous, and conformist is the only way they feel they can be loved, since others seem stronger and more capable. "Besides, nobody's interested in what I think or say," Mary, twenty-five, says.

□ *The Martyrs* believe they will be loved only if they please and serve everybody. They complain when their full-time sacrifices go unappreciated, but pleasing others is what life is all about, isn't it? This is what their parents expected them to do, and they carried their parents' expectations into their adult lives. "If I go out of my way all the time to help people, they will love me in return," Mabel, forty-one, says.

□ *The Drifters* passively receive each day's largesse or disappointment. Making things happen for the better is something other people do, for they learned long ago that their attempts to affect the world around them were doomed to failure. Mom and Dad treated them as if they were pieces of furniture. Any love or affection their parents gave them was an accidental treat. "It's the breaks. Finding someone to love is like being in a crap game and hitting a lucky seven," Henry, thirty-six, says.

□ *The Yesterdayers* found growing up scary and disappointing when they discovered they themselves would have to fill the enormous dependency needs Mom and Dad filled for them in earlier life. Love meant being indulged. They were Mom and Dad's cute little girl or manly boy who could do no wrong. Their whims were always satisfied and they were never disciplined. Passive response was all that was required to attain love. Grown-up life, on the other hand, demands their active participation, something life never prepared them for. Consequently, they retreat into the past. For them yesterday is always better than today; and the farther back in the past that yesterday is, the rosier it seems in the light of the demands the present makes on them. "They don't make women today like my mother," Jim, thirty-five, says.

□   *The Futurizers* are the mirror images of the yester-dayers. They learned to survive the pain of insufficient love in their earlier years by believing that today is not important. It's what will happen tomorrow that counts. "Love is just around the corner. I'm waiting for Mr. Right.—one day soon, he's going to show up," says Janet, twenty-eight.

□   *The Me-Firsters* learned early that life is a jungle and that nice guys finish last, because niceness is weakness; to trust anyone is to be hurt in return. Deception and force decide who is to survive. People are objects to be manipulated with guile and contempt, because, like me-firsters, they were lovelessly dealt with when they were growing up. Their parents were always untrustworthy; the promised birthday presents never materialized; and Mom said she loved them but that was just an excuse she used to get them to do the chores she wanted done. "All women try to con you into marriage or a living-together arrangement. No way!" Don, thirty-four, says.

□   *The Erasers* grew up escaping problems by erasing them. Problems will vanish if they are not seen or heard. The violent arguments between their parents were so painful they had to be blocked out of their consciousness. They are the people, like Amy, forty-three, who say truthfully in great bewilderment, "But I never saw anything wrong; I thought we were both happy the last fifteen years," when a spouse asks for a divorce because he felt those fifteen years were excruciatingly dull. And that bewilderment of "never having seen anything wrong" recurs at the end of each new post-divorce relationship, since they have never taken off their blindfolds and earplugs.

□ *The Agonizers* derive meaning out of life from worrying twenty-four hours a day over what they have done or might do. Childhood was the time when nothing was certain and nobody could be counted on for security: They never knew if they'd be hugged or slapped, fussed over or rejected. How could they trust people to be "there" when they needed them, particularly the people they loved? "He said he wanted to see me this Friday, but I know from the tone of his voice he didn't really want to—or did he?" Alice, twenty-seven, says.

□ *The Wallowers* are close relatives of the agonizers. They comfort themselves by believing that self-pity is the only balm for the slings and arrows that come their way. Their self-pity is a poor substitute for lack of love in their earliest years. To tell them their life isn't so bad is to risk the inevitable reply that Andy, thirty-two, gives: "But you don't know how really bad it is. Let me tell you about the date who walked out on me last night."

□ *The Controllers* fear behavior they can't control. Their parents taught them that love was a scarce commodity only to be earned by a nice little girl or boy who never got angry, never dirtied clothes. Spontaneity was a punishable offense. Super-organized orderliness, control of feelings and relationships, list-making predictability for today, tomorrow, and forever is how their parents taught them to love. One step in a new direction is seen as a step toward chaos. They have banished the possibility that chance and adventure could enrich their lives. "But I can't do that—I've never called up a man before he called me in my life. It just wouldn't be me if I did that," Sally, thirty-seven, says.

□ *The Shoulders* believe they can't possibly be loved for themselves. Their natural feelings were considered bad if they conflicted with Mom's and Dad's conceptions about how they "should" think, feel, and act. To win love and approval, they conformed to their parents' ideas of right and wrong. "I've done all the right things, so why should all my relationships turn as sour as they always do?" Maria, thirty-nine, says.

□ *The Righteously Angry* feel they were cheated of sufficient love when they were young. They were always second best; brothers and sisters got more attention than they did. The fact that no one recognized their worth left a pool of angry feelings inside them. "Why does every woman I go out with tell me I'm too demanding and touchy? It's because they are ignorant and self-centered—that's why," Rod, forty-five, erupts.

□ *The Resentment Collectors* feel their parents forced them into a mold. If they were boys, they would be loved if they never cried. If they were girls, they won affection by being nice and never angry. They stored up, but never expressed, the resentment they felt at not being permitted to express their feelings. "Now that my last relationship has ended, I can see she pissed me off in so many ways it's a wonder I stayed in it as long as I did. Her attitudes and interests never appealed to me, but I just went along not saying anything because I thought things might improve on their own," Walter, twenty-eight, says.

Your Yes-Buts may result from your having learned to love in the above ways. Your earliest experiences of what you think love is and how you can get it provide you with the spectacles through which you may be seeing and interpreting your relation to yourself and others today. Since a child lacks the experience to interpret his or her world accurately, distortions are built into the lenses of these spectacles. Perhaps you are still seeing your current situations through the distorted lenses of your childhood without being aware of the fact. To see if you may need to substitute undistorted adult lenses to resolve your Yes-But dilemma, ask yourself the following questions:

□ Do you believe you are worthy of being loved?

□ Do you believe you have only a limited number of qualities others will consider lovable?

□ Do you have a fixed image of yourself as the kind of person who can love only in certain ways?

Of course, if you were asked these questions in the company of others, it is likely that you would put your best face forward and answer politely or evade answering. However, when you meditate on these questions in a safe environment, a room in which you are alone with yourself, other more authentic answers may be forthcoming. It is the rare person indeed who won't honestly acknowledge in privacy that he or she has grave reservations about his or her capacity to love and trust more than one type of person. In addition, fear about ever being fully accepted as lovable, and anxiety that parts of yourself are unlovable and must be hidden from others, may surface inside. The child you were may still be alive and kicking in your present feelings about yourself. Who has ever felt he or she ever received the fullest amount of love, trust, care, tenderness, affection, and concern he or she hoped for from those earliest very special persons? It is normal and natural to feel this way. One would have to search far and wide to find a person who honestly felt that he or she had been fully accepted in their childhood years for what they were as human beings and not what was expected of them. Who has not felt that he or she could only survive and obtain the love of their parents by conforming to an image of themselves that contradicted their own needs and feelings?

These early learned impressions can impact on our adult personalities in the self-defeating ways they do on the men and women with the personality types discussed earlier. Locked-in positions have to be given up before new opportunities can arise:

□ When the *Externalizers* become aware that a new wig or a five-pound weight loss does not bring forth a lasting love relationship, they may find themselves attracting people who like the reality of who they are rather than what they pretend to be.

□ When the *Don't-Make-Wavers* understand that their unassertiveness turns people off, they may assert themselves and find themselves more appreciated.

□ When the *Martyrs* discover that pleasing others at the expense of themselves creates stored-up resentment that shows in their behavior, they can attract new kinds of people.

□ When the *Drifters* realize they are no longer Mom and Dad's captives, and that they can make independent decisions that can effectively present their personalities to others, attaining new relationships will no longer be a matter of luck.

□   When the *Yesterdayers* recognize that nursing the past is a security blanket that only guarantees the "safety" of no new relationships happening in their life, then living in the present can become a challenge to expand relationships rather than a threat to the memories they hold so dear.

□   When the *Futurizers* find that it is what they do *today* that will determine whether or not tomorrow is bright, they may begin to see the opportunities for new relationships that were always present.

□   When the *Me-Firsters* see that their contempt for others reflects the hatred they feel for themselves and that loving others is a sign of strength rather than weakness, life can become more than just a series of one-night stands.

□   When the *Erasers* see that denying difficult realities leads to the ending of relationships rather than their continuance, they can begin to improve the quality of their relationships by recognizing and dealing straightforwardly with the problems.

□   When the *Agonizers* understand that no one but themselves can give them the guidelines for living they seek from others, new possibilities for better relationships can materialize.

□   When the *Wallowers* see that fertilizing their past can only create a desert out of their present life, old losses will be cut and new gains will prove to be possible.

□   When the *Controllers* realize that life is uncertain, they can see in each new day new possibilities for improving the quality of their relationships rather than for reconfirming past rejections.

□   When the *Shoulders* learn that accepting their own

feelings will help them to have healthier relationships with others, good relationships will follow.

□   When the *Righteously Angry* understand that anger inevitably alienates people, that they must first deal with their own fears and flaws, which they ascribe to others, they can then radiate attention and caring to receptive others.

□   When the *Resentment Collectors* recognize that resentment creates the dust that blinds their eyes to the friendly signals other people are sending out to them, they can become alert to those signals and respond in kind.

TAKING OFF YOUR BEST-FACE-FORWARD MASK

Fear is the jailer that keeps us locked up in Yes-Buts, fear of who we think we ''really'' are. While we want love and intimacy in the form of a special person to enter our life, we also fear it might really happen! It is the feeling of be-careful-about-what-you-want-you're-liable-to-get-it. We consciously and truly want that love and intimacy, but a hidden part of ourself is saying in the way we act to others: ''Don't see me as I think I really am, because under my surface you will find I'm not worthy of the love of a person I value.''

As I write this, I am reminded of Elaine, an attractive, thirtyish woman whose complaint had been the Yes-But of always finding herself in shallow relationships. Once she became aware that she was seeking those relationships out of her own fear, she was then able to see she was looking at every new potential for love through the distorted lenses of her childhood:

"My parents were very close to each other, but they shut out everyone else," she said. "They showed very little affection for me and my two older sisters. I thought there must be something wrong with me because they didn't hug and kiss me or pay me any attention. I felt I was a total disappointment to them. I didn't have too much confidence in my own values and I guess I had the fear that if anyone really got attracted to me they would be fooled. Because if they *really* knew who I was, they wouldn't want any part of me. How could they when I didn't feel good about myself? So in order to keep a relationship, I would have to create the illusion that I was bright and more interesting than I thought I was. I even went so far as to break off an engagement with a very special man because I was sure that someone that fantastic could not possibly love me once we started to live together and he really got to know me. Instead I sought out somebody that I felt I deserved, because I was too afraid to marry that fantastic guy. And what I thought I deserved was a man who put me down and told me what to do all the time. That was the kind of a guy I married, since it was better than not getting any attention at all. But what a rotten bargain I got. I see now I set it all up. But in the four years since my divorce, I continue to get into relationships that I end first if I find myself getting too close to men who really appeal to me. Or I'm bored to tears with the turkeys who say they are turned on by me and press for more of my time. I'm more and more aware of what I am doing, but I'm having such a hard time dropping it."

Elaine is further along toward springing herself out of her Yes-But jail than she yet realizes. She still perpetuates the common illusion that change for the better comes easy. She has still to learn that old habits of loving die hard. Those old habits are not divorce-related, but have been living inside her since her earliest years. New habits can be substituted, but they should be expected under those circumstances to come haltingly, awkwardly, and in bits and pieces instead of over-night.

As Terry, a woman who was nodding in vigorous agreement with Elaine, pointed out, "You know, Elaine, I found out it takes time. I know I learned to feel inadequate over a long period, but I'm changing with one step at a time now. The important thing is that you know now what you have been doing to yourself. You are no longer that little girl so you can change. You no longer have to buy the trip your parents placed on you and that you placed on yourself. After all, you come across in this group as a very bright, warm, lively lady. All you have to do is to show your true self, not the neglected child you once were. Then things will happen for the better. They won't happen overnight, but they'll happen."

The important new development in Elaine's life that affords her the possibility of positive change is the fact that she has gotten in touch with her basic fear that she is un-worthy of being loved by any "fantastic" person, someone she values and respects. She now knows that she *learned* to feel that way in the family environment in which she grew up. As long as she was unaware that those past feelings were controlling the present way she relates to men, she would remain in her Yes-But jail no matter how many new men she meets. However, she can now begin to see herself as she exists today, not as she existed in her earlier years. The more she gets in touch with the fact that she is a valuable person, capable of being loved for who she is today, the more she will send out signals to the kind of men she does not have to play any games with. She will be able to love a person she values and make a commitment to him when she begins to see herself as a lovable and valuable grown-up person instead of as a vulnerable child. Since she learned to be "unworthy" of love, she can now learn to be worthy of love by seeing herself as a woman with a potential for change and personal growth in the present.

The basic fear that Elaine honestly expressed is at the core of all Yes-But complaints. And men are held captive by that fear, too. Dustin, a man of Elaine's age, reacted to Elaine's experience as follows:

"I recently met a striking-looking blonde woman at a party. I liked her immediately; she was real warm, alive, and outgoing. After the party we went and had a cup of coffee and I took her home and got her phone number. I didn't try to make out; it just felt good getting to know her. But after I left, I started to think—'Why would she want to go out with me?' Yes, I feel that way often."

This basic fear of being an unworthy person who will be rejected by someone we care about if our mask is removed defeats the possibility of a new, lasting love relationship. It is only natural for us to want to feel good about ourselves and to have others validate us as being worthy of respect and love. However, when we think aspects of ourselves are unacceptable to others because we thought they were unacceptable to the parents we loved, self-defeat is the end result. For how can we receive the unconditional love of another person, and respond in kind, if down deep we fear we may be unlovable? To protect ourselves as best we can against the humiliation, hurt, and pain of possible rejection, we often will reject the other person in an unrealistic anticipation that he or she will reject us first.

We put what we think is our best face forward in each new relationship in order to disguise the unacceptable person we think we may be behind our mask. Perhaps you yourself may be wearing one or more of these masks every time you meet a new person in the hope that the mask will attract affection and love:

☐ *The What-a-Great-Person-I-Am Mask*

The person who claims to have accomplished everything and tells about it nonstop detail all evening long. Admiration is assumed to be forthcoming.

☐ *The Fun-Person Mask*

The life-of-the-party, play-the-clown person who thinks that perpetual liveliness will win interest and commitment. "I'm funny, therefore I'm desirable," is the plea behind the clowning.

☐ *The Broken-Wing Mask*

The helpless woman who needs a big, strong man to take charge of her life. And the helpless man searching for "Big Mamma" to take care of him. Love is to be attained by making the other person feel strong.

☐ *The Mender-of-Broken-Wings Mask*

The man who gains affection by doing an endless variety of things, solicited and unsolicited, for any woman he finds attractive. The woman who is absorbed in nurturing every need, real or imagined, of the man with whom she hopes to maintain a relationship.

□   *The Strong-Silent Mask*

The person who takes charge without consulting the other person, under the impression that such forcefulness is admirable; and who says little or nothing in the belief that silence comes across as thoughtfulness and attractiveness.

□   *The Total-Honesty Mask*

The person who tells the entire story of his or her life, all problems included, at the first date, under the impression that people admire and are enticed by indiscriminate openness.

□   *The All-Things-to-All-People Mask*

The person who convinces himself or herself to like only what the other person in the relationship likes, and who tries to become what the other person wants even though that may violate his or her sense of self. Love and affection is to be gained through the giving up of one's personality.

□   *The Exotic Mask*

The man or woman who gains attention through shock and surprise. Far-out clothing, hot-tub parties, the latest fashionable drug habit are the assumed ways to another person's heart.

□   *The Across-the-Crowded-Room Mask*

The man or woman who has fallen in love with love so that every new person is pressed too close, too fast. Ardent professions of passion are vowed an hour after a first introduction in the belief that such intense attention will elicit a similar response.

□   *The Profit-and-Loss Mask*

The man or woman who shows how sensible, secure, and reliable he or she is, leaving the impression with the other person that love is security and safety, to the exclusion of everything else.

□   *The Sexual-Athlete Mask*

The man or woman who talks of love as if that meant a new coital position every night. The promise of outstanding erections or exquisite multiple orgasms is offered in the hope of eliciting admiration and affection.

□   *The Intellectual-Athlete Mask*

The man or woman who proudly and instantly announces he or she has read and seen everything. Brilliance of mind and talk, talk, talk are felt to be the essence of lovability. The intellectual athlete misplaces the heart above the neck, in contrast to the sexual athlete who locates a person's heart below the belt.

□   *The Passionate-Sports-Person Mask*

The person who believes skill in a particular sport means personal worth. Athletic prowess is all these people feel they have to offer.

Best-face-forward masks are always self-defeating. They end your chance of getting to know a person better instead of encouraging that possibility. When people try to gain your interest with a best-face-forward mask, there always seems to be an atmosphere of strain, artificiality, anxiety, and tension. Without meaning to, that person has turned you off instead of on.

If you find yourself continually frustrated by an inability to connect positively with a person of the opposite sex, consider the possibility that you may be putting on a best-face-forward mask for others. When it comes to wanting to love and be loved, all men and women are the same. All of us want someone to like us for all the qualities we possess. But we may fear that only a part of us is truly lovable. If as a child we felt we were loved only for our sports prowess or entertainment value or conformity or inconspicuousness or report card A's, the traces of that past will continue to influence our present behavior. As Fran, a woman who wore a mender-of-broken-wings mask, told me, "I was loved for making the beds, doing the dishes, and watching after my baby brother, but never for *me*. And that's what I still do with every guy I meet; I try to take care of him. My ex is an alcoholic and I'm always meeting new alcoholics who tell me how lovable I am. But the men I find attractive don't seem to respond to me."

MELTING YOUR FROZEN LOVE IMAGE

You want to be liked, so you put what you think is your best face forward. But that aspect turns the person you are attracted to off. You feel like you are at a dead end. You can only get out of the dead end by melting your frozen love image. For when it comes to the need for love and intimacy, the child in each of us has never died. Because that need is so deeply rooted within us from birth, it is bound to be a potent force as long as we live. During the first few years after a divorce that need is like a banked fire. But when it is ready to flare up again after other priorities have been resolved successfully in a creative divorce, most people react as if they were not the competent adults they are in the many other areas of their life.

But a frozen love image can be melted and a mature love image can take its place. Here are the steps the men and women in my Learning to Love Again Seminars have found helpful in making that substitution:

Step 1: See your situation in a new light.

Acknowledge to yourself that your old ways of relating have not helped you better your relationships with the opposite sex. React to this admission not with a sense of hopelessness and of being a personal "failure." View it instead as a consequence of being unaware that you learned to love in self-defeating ways early in life. If you have learned the wrong ways, you can *now* learn the right ways by becoming aware that right ways exist.

Step 2: React to the present as the present.

View each new person in your life that you might be attracted to as an opportunity, not as a threat. Today you are a cause as well as an effect. You have enormous power to influence the impression you make on a person you are attracted to. You do this by the way you act and react to that person. How you act and react will increase or diminish the other person's interest in you. Continuing to see yourself as a "victim" will only invite further victimization.

Step 3: Differentiate between love learned in childhood and adult love.

Love learned in childhood sees the person you love solely as the extension of your needs. You are perpetuating childhood reaction if:

a) You view the person you are attracted to as an object to be attained. You think of what the other person *must* give you, rather than what both of you can freely give each other.

b) You insist on love on demand. Because you are attracted to another person, you want instant acceptance with the same intensity you are feeling. If you don't get an immediate emotional return, you feel totally rejected.

c) You see relationships in terms of winning or losing: Getting a date is being a "success," not having one, a "failure." Leaving a singles affair with someone is "scoring," leaving alone is being a "loser."

d) You define love as fiery excitement of immediate physical attraction, to the exclusion of other qualities. When the flame sputters out, you are completely disillusioned.

e) You look for the perfect person. You expect Mr. Right or Ms. Right to appear out of nowhere and give you the oceans of love you feel you are entitled to receive, to make up for the lack of love in your earlier years.

f) You do not permit a relationship to proceed at its own pace and develop over time. The new people in your life are always judged and found wanting at the end of a first or second date. You see the other person not as himself or herself. You always compare the other person with your idea of Mr. or Ms. Right.

Step 4: Learn to identify your I-have-been-here-before feelings.

Notice the way you may be reacting to each new person as if he or she were people from your past rather than individuals in your present. The way a person may laugh or talk or sit, the color of his or her eyes or hair, his or her likes or dislikes may remind you negatively or positively of someone you used to know. Those I-have-been-here-before feelings may make you misjudge the new person in your life, who is unique, just as you are. I-have-been-here-before feelings are powerful because you are unaware of their presence. They are like an invisible third party at a table for two whispering to you how to react to the new person you are facing. If you become aware that these feelings may arise when you meet a new person, you can discount the distorted judgments they insinuate in your ears. "He is just like . . ." or "she reminds me of . . ." are the favorite phrases I-have-been-here-before feelings use to make themselves heard.

Step 5: Cultivate receptiveness.

Permit people to come into your life instead of giving them double signals. Choose between protecting yourself against hurt and your desire for a lasting love relationship. Recognize that intimacy *always* involves the possibility of rejection, since not everybody you like will like you in return. Nor will everyone who is attracted to you always be the person you like. The person with an adult love image understands that there is a price to be paid for intimacy. The price is high, but that is because the rewards are so very high.

Step 6: Connect with the universality of your feelings.

Remember that you are not alone: Your basic need for acceptance and love, and your basic fear of rejection, are part of being human! Every man and woman has that same need and that same fear. Reminding yourself that the person you are attempting to know better has needs and fears too will make it easier for you to discard your best-face-forward mask and allow your total personality to emerge. Eve brought the following poem to share with her LTLA group.

She found it an aid in cultivating her receptiveness; perhaps
you will too:

Don't Be Fooled by Me!

Don't be fooled by me.
Don't be fooled by the face I wear.
For I wear a thousand masks, masks that I'm afraid to take
off.
For none of them are me.

Pretending is an art that is second nature with me, but don't
be fooled—for God's sake, don't be fooled.
I give the impression that I'm secure
that all is sunny and unruffled with me,
within as well as without,
that confidence is my name and coolness my game;
that the water's calm and I'm in command,
and that I need no one.
But don't believe me. Please.

My surface may seem smooth, but my surface is my mask
Beneath lies no complacence
Beneath dwells the real me in confusion, in fear and
aloneness.
But I hide this. I don't want anybody to know it.
I panic at the thought of my weakness and fear of being
exposed.
That's why I frantically create a mask to hide behind,
a nonchalant, sophisticated facade.
to help me pretend, to shield me from the glance that knows.
But such a glance is precisely my salvation. My only
salvation,

and I know it.
That is, if it's followed by acceptance, if it's followed by love.
It's the only thing that will assure me of what I can't assure
myself—that I am worth something.

But I don't tell you this. I don't dare. I'm afraid to.
I'm afraid your glance will not be followed by acceptance
*   and love.*
I'm afraid you'll think less of me, that you'll laugh at me,
and your laugh would kill me.
I'm afraid that deep down I'm nothing, that I'm no good
and that you will see this and reject me.
So I play my game, my desperate game,
with a façade of assurance without and a trembling child
*   within.*
So begins the parade of masks—and my life becomes a front.

Who am I, you may wonder. I am someone you know very
*   well.*
For I am every man you meet and I am every woman you
*   meet.*

When you melt your frozen love image, your Yes-Buts
will no longer appear to be overwhelming obstacles to new
relationships. You will be able to use your eleven lifelines to
learning to love to offer yourself realistic hope in place of
frustration and despair. You will be able to create new
possibilities for a lasting love relationship to happen, as the
next chapter will demonstrate.

4 Readiness Time: The Four Stages of Learning to Love Again

Letting go of the childhood-based way of seeing yourself as a person with limited love possibilities will free you from your Yes-But bind. Yes-Buts can now become challenges for you to react differently to the situations you are presently experiencing.

Viewing your Yes-Buts in the light of the present reality of who you are will enable you to discover that *Yes-Buts are the disguises that a new beginning wears*. Your feelings that you are at a dead end, that you are frustrated by outside events and doomed to repeat unsatisfactory activities, are really evidence that you want to take a step forward instead of backward. You can wallow in these feelings; you can run away from them only to meet them again in the loneliness of your bedroom. Or you can try to make new and more positive relationships happen in your life.

To be sick and tired of being sick and tired of hearing

yourself complain about the lack of a lasting love relationship in your life is the readiness fuel you need to make a fresh start. But you must determine what you are indeed ready for. June, a thirty-two-year-old woman, remarked to me, "I find that I've gone from crisis to complacency. That first year of my divorce was absolute hell. But now that I'm three years out of my marriage, things have settled down and I like my freedom. I don't have trouble meeting people. I date a lot of different men and am selective about whom I go to bed with. Lately, however, I get twinges of yearning for a close relationship with someone special, someone I wish would come into my life. But that scares me a little—I'm not prepared to give up my freedom. I feel sort of guilty about wanting another monogamous relationship because it would swallow me up."

Many not-so-recently divorced men and women find themselves saying the same things June is saying. If you hear the same thoughts running through your mind, trust their wisdom. They are telling you that you may not be ready yet to make a close commitment happen. There is still unfinished business in your life to resolve. As long as you think a close relationship is more of a threat than a promise, you will distance people from you. This is precisely what June was doing. In her LTLA group she continually voiced Yes-Buts that proclaimed she could not meet any really interesting or attractive men who were not married and that the men she met were only interested in shallow relationships.

Men are no different from women in this respect. I can recall four men who loudly proclaimed in an LTLA group two years ago that they enjoyed playing the field and that all the woman they met were trying to get their hooks into them, manipulate and dominate them, just like their former wives did. A close monogamous commitment? Remarriage? "No way!" was their vehement response. It is now two years later and two of these four are now involved in monogamous living-together arrangements, while the other two have re-married. They met the women they are presently relating to in a constructive way after their vigorous denial of their need for a close relationship. They could only do so when they were ready in their mind and feelings to make such a commit-ment. Before that time, their Yes-Buts served as protective coatings. They performed the positive function of preventing these men from making too early, rash commitments. Yes-Buts gave them the time and distance to melt their frozen love images and connect with their eleven lifelines to learning to love again.

To recognize that your Yes-Buts are likely to be per-forming a positive function in your life rather than a negative one is to take a giant step on the road toward learning to love again. In effect, they can be saying to you, "Proceed at your own pace, don't let external pressures move you to a stage you don't feel ready for, give yourself the time and distance to see yourself and your opportunities in a new light." It is only when you wallow in Yes-Buts and repeat ways of behaving long after you've given yourself the message that such behavior produces unsatisfying results that Yes-Buts become barriers to learning to love again. And when you are sick and tired of being sick and tired of what you see you are doing to yourself, you will be receptive to constructive new ideas and approaches to your dealings with the opposite sex. The balance within yourself will then shift from a need for stability to a desire to risk the new.

In previous chapters I have indicated that learning to love again means learning to love in new, adult ways. It means establishing a new kind of relationship within yourself as a precondition for establishing a fulfilling relationship with another person. It means learning from your past ways of relating rather than repeating those past ways. It means tapping the wisdom in your past experience rather than remembering the past as a dump heap of failures and mistakes. It means stretching yourself to constructively influence the course of your relationships rather than limiting your capabilities for doing so out of self-complacency or fear. To assume that these necessary conditions for building more satisfying relationships will come easily or overnight is just as naïve and self-defeating as it is to assume that a divorce from an agonizingly sour marriage instantly in and of itself solves all the problems in life. Even if you intellectually acknowledge to yourself that these conditions for building new relationships are indeed desirable, they will produce effective results for you only if you apply and experience their meaning in your daily life. Otherwise all you will be doing is reading the words in this book as a substitute for taking action rather than as a spur to action.

In the lived experience of your creative divorce you have already firmed up the eleven learning-to-love-again lifeline resources within you to successfully take this next step in your growth as a human being capable of loving and being loved. However, something else is also needed before you can chart a new direction for yourself. What is needed are signposts along the new pathway you will be traveling that can enable you to risk acting, thinking, and feeling in new ways, signposts that can sustain the sense of loss you may feel in letting go of old ways without any advance guarantee that the new ways "must" prove successful, signposts that can assist you in weathering the inevitable setbacks and resurgences of frustration, anxiety, and hopelessness that come with chancing the new. For as Dr. John Enright has well said about the hesitations people feel about taking steps in a new direction:

> It's like the man with his hands full of weevily peanuts who sees a T-bone steak across the room. He knows there's protein in the peanuts, but he would rather have the steak. Yet, to get the steak he must drop the peanuts. For a brief time he knows his hands will be empty. How can he be sure he will get the steak? He knows the peanuts are real; maybe the steak is a mirage. And so he stays, unhappy with his peanuts, longing for the steak, but afraid to take the risk of letting go.

There are, fortunately, signposts along the way that can enable you to give up the peanuts because the steak is very real. Those signposts can be identified as the Four Developmental Stages of Learning to Love Again. Just as there were stages of development you had to live through in your own divorce (such as separation shock, the mourning process, the establishment of your single-person identity) in order to make it a creative experience, so too new and equally significant developmental stages must be lived through in order to attain a lasting love relationship. Each stage is a way station on the road to the achievement of that end. Your creative divorce was the result of a voyage of discovery about yourself and other people that you had to proceed with at your own pace. Similarly, you will determine the time when you are internally ready to experience each new stage of your learning-to-love-again journey. The positive function of your Yes-Buts, as I will subsequently show in this chapter, is that they are the signals alerting you to identify and evaluate the stage of learning to love again that you are currently experiencing. They are also the jolts you need to propel you to the next and more fulfilling stage of your love development. However, Yes-Buts can be used in this positive fashion only if you are first aware of, identify, and understand the meaning of these four *new* stages in your life. Here are the stages and the special characteristics of each of them:

STAGE ONE: THE REMEMBERED-PAIN STAGE

In this first stage any thought of a lasting love relationship feels like salt poured on an open wound. "Don't come close to me; I've been hurt too much," is the signal one sends out to the opposite sex. Feelings of being a half-person predominate now that the marriage has been severed. The divorce is still too recent and too painful. One manufactures cocoons of self-imposed isolation, self-pity, and possible overindulgence in alcohol or uppers and downers as protections against a hostile world. Every couple walking by is seen as an accusation against oneself: "You are an outcast because you have failed and are guilty of the crime of no longer being a part of a couple. The world is a Noah's Ark from which you are now barred because you are single."

Sometimes alternating with self-imposed isolation are wild swings in the opposite direction. The desire to marry immediately someone "better" than one's ex-spouse, the desire to belong *to* someone so that one is taken care of—these are the yearnings of the half-person. The idea that a relationship based on belonging *with* another person, because one is already a whole person, is not entertained at this stage.

How long does this stage last? It may last a few weeks, a few months, a few years, or a lifetime, depending on the individual. Every man or woman has an *individual* timetable based on his or her self-awareness and personal motivation to move into the new. Typically, however, the healthy thrust for personal growth surfaces up within each man and woman within a year after separation and they are ready for the next stage.

STAGE TWO: THE QUESTING-EXPERIMENTAL STAGE

This is the time of dawning emotional recognition that one is indeed a single person who has the opportunity to respond to the new challenges of divorced life in new ways. The pull of the past and the remembered pain of the breakup of the closest commitment in life is still present but it diminishes in intensity. The realization that one now has the freedom to make new acquaintanceships and friendships and act on that freedom emerges.

It is a time of discovering one is not alone—that being

divorced means one is joining the ranks of millions of others in a similar stage. New support systems and a new sense of community are seen to exist (singles church groups, singles adjustment groups, etc.). The healthy need to connect with new people pushes itself forward. But one feels very fragile, very fearful: How to relate to others now that I am no longer a wife or a husband? Am I attractive? Will new people desire me, want me, need me? Who would possibly want to get involved with a reject, a loser, a failure like me? These are the questions that are plaguing one's mind at this time. Yet the normal human need to reconnect with others is more powerful than the fears, and one begins to try out one's new freedom. But where to go? And what to do when one gets there? The first response usually is to rush out to singles bars or singles organizations as if driven to them because the loneliness is overwhelming. In those places new connections may be made, but they are very shallow, tentative, short-lived, distancing. And sex becomes the greatest distancer of all. Promiscuity for the time being becomes the name of the game. The double standard is ending in America, so one finds more and more women as well as men opting for this game. A warm body in bed is believed to be better than nothing; at least it's a protection against the terrors of a lonely night. Out of the need to feel needed, indiscriminate bed-jumping seems to temporarily prove to oneself that one is indeed an attractive, valuable person. But sooner or later (typically sooner), sex experienced only as release of tension and physical performance becomes strangely unsatisfying, even boring. Suddenly sex without affection, tenderness, or caring for each other doesn't answer one's needs the way one expected it to.

But at this stage any close commitment to another person based on mutual respect and equality and caring is still inconceivable. One still feels too damaged. Better to remain noninvolved personally, if involved physically. However, even physiological satisfaction proves to be not worth extended effort. Another night on the town with someone good in bed but whose name you can't even remember the next morning—is it really worth it? Why not just stay home for a change—read a book, be quiet, or masturbate if the sex urge is that pressing? These questions begin to substitute for the earlier belief that sex and more sex is the answer to one's difficulties. Soon after this awareness surfaces, new behavior occurs. One chooses to be alone at times rather than feel compelled to escape into the flesh of the next woman or man you "must" meet. Sex as a form of exploitation —of using someone or being used—has diminished in appeal.

All during this stage the signal one sends out to others is: "Come no closer than one inch toward me. Can't you see how super-sensitive, vulnerable, and defiant I am? I am available only as a body—and so are you. Don't ask for anything more because I have nothing more to give." When this signal diminishes one is ready for the next stage of development. Many men and women experience this readiness within less than two years after their divorce. However, just as in Stage One, you are the determiner of your own readiness, which may be more or less than the two-year span. There is no right or wrong time, there is only the time that fits for you.

STAGE THREE: THE SELECTIVE-DISTANC-ING STAGE

This is the time when the belief that one is a half-person begins to diminish. A sense of one's competence as a single individual capable of taking more effective charge of one's life begins to emerge. The fear of not being able to survive on one's own and the compulsive, indiscriminate need to be needed by anyone and everyone have passed. The hassles with the ex-spouse and the legal wrangles have pretty well ended. Now the desire for new relationships begins to feel more like a promise of adventure rather than a guarantee of new pain and new rejection.

The self-discovery of being able to constructively survive as a single person enables one to risk a new kind of involvement with the opposite sex. It is an involvement that is more selective than those in the previous stage: The kind of people one wants to relate to assumes a greater importance. Going out with just anyone for the sake of going out, in order to prove one's self-worth, has lost its appeal since one is feeling better about oneself. Instead of daily and desperately seeking out a one-night-stand partner, the option of staying home alone is exercised more frequently. Or calling up or visiting with a friend of the same sex surprisingly proves to be more gratifying than a fleeting body in bed. "What's the value if the person I physically connect with doesn't appeal to me as a human being? Why waste the time? Wouldn't it be nice to meet someone who is interesting, with whom I can share experiences, and who can turn me on as well?" These are the questions pressing for answer at this stage of development.

Raising these questions propels one to new behavior. The absence of a Saturday-night date no longer gives rise to the panic-stricken anxiety that one is abandoned, rejected, and therefore worthless. The time alone becomes a time for making friends with oneself instead of a time of waiting until the telephone rings. And when the telephone does ring and the person asking for a date is unlikable or dull, one can turn the request down, since reading, listening to records, or writing letters seems a more pleasant alternative.

In this stage the impulse to reach out for new acquaintances, friends, and longer lasting relationships arises from a greater sense of inner security. One realizes that there may be interesting people "out there" who would like to know you as much as you would like to know them. One begins to make oneself available to meet those new people in more and more places—at work, through friends, through the pursuit of hobbies, at parties, at lectures, workshops, and courses in continuing education, in political and social organizations. Or at chance encounters in a museum, along a bicycle path, and even in an elevator or supermarket.

As one gets to know more people, a sorting-out process takes place. Running through one's mind are thoughts like: "*This* person makes me feel comfortable and could be a friend, *that* person turns me off, while *this other* person is attractive and interesting so maybe a potential for some kind of intimate relationship is present. . . ." It is easier to make friends now, but gaining a closer commitment with a person of the opposite sex presents difficulties. Many of these difficulties are self-created, because in this stage of development mixed feelings predominate. The longer one experiences this stage the more intense becomes the longing for a lasting love relationship with one special person. But the fear that such a close commitment will inevitably end in disaster, just as previous close commitments have, is also very much alive. The healthy urge to meet and totally commit oneself to loving a special person clashes with the fear that should this *actually* happen the result would prove disastrous. Anxiety mounts up in one's belief that a horrendously painful breakup will be the inevitable consequence of a commitment. One's feelings scream, "Since that happened before, it *must* happen again. So don't place too much trust in anyone!"

However, the need for a special relationship proves too strong to be ignored and must be acted on. But how to protect oneself against the remembered pain of past "failures"? A compromise—like trying to eat one's cake and have it too—is worked out within oneself. In order to get the goodies that can only come from a close commitment, without paying the imagined price of being hurt as a result of obtaining them, one establishes distancing relationships. The signal one sends to others in this stage is: "Come-close-but-go-away-because-I-don't-want-to-be-hurt-again."

Closer relations are indeed attained. Instead of the self-imposed isolation and desperate promiscuity manifested in Stages One and Two, selective relationships are established. Compatability of personality, background, and life experiences may become more important in the choice of whom one goes out with than sex for the sake of sex. But one is not prepared to share totally who one is with the people one dates. Fear of being rejected again still hovers in the background. The new relationships tend therefore to be short-lived; one tends to reject the other person before he or she does the rejecting. Three-date affairs or four-week living-together arrangements, involvement in two- or three-month romances that begin with instant, powerful attraction and end with disillusionment are typical in this stage. Coming on too close-too fast occurs frequently—at least one can feel the passion and aliveness of connecting with a love object, if only for a short time.

Many people in this stage open up only a small crack in the protective wall against possible future hurt that they have built around themselves. Some find it impossible to sustain a relationship after two or three dates with a person. They have no difficulty in meeting people, but continually find themselves at the end of a relationship before it even develops. Others have shopping lists in their heads that screen out practically all potential relationships. The lists are usually composed of lengthy qualifications and requirements that no other person could possibly meet in their entirety. While they wait for that perfect person on the shopping list, they distance themselves from the very people who have the potential for becoming lasting love partners.

A number of men and women in this stage try to hedge their bets while they wait for that perfect person by adopting "standbys." They think of standbys as nice, but second-best, people, usually available when needed—for protection against loneliness, for limited sharing and caring, for some possible sex. Standbys are more than just friends, but will always be less than lovers. Standbys are "there" for when an affair with someone else breaks up or when companionship is needed to fill an empty evening. Hovering over one's head in standby relationships is the feeling that something is less-than-satisfying about the nature of the connection. In addition, one may experience twinges of guilt from the feeling that one is "using" the standby person.

Sooner or later in this third stage, the balance of forces inside oneself tips in favor of a new long-lasting close commitment. The courage to chance a new intimate relationship is greater than the fear of its possible failure. One begins to believe that the new relationship does not *necessarily* have to end in failure and rejection. The new holds the possibility of being something more than just a repetition of the past.

When does this happen? You can't set any time limits for this stage any more than you could set a limit for the previous stages. The desire for a lasting love relationship is normal to most people and I have seen it frequently emerge after two or three years of living single. But it can and does happen at surprising times. You may be ready to act on the realization that this is what you want and need, and are willing to risk making it happen, five years or longer after your divorce. Whatever the time element involved, once your readiness is established, one is ready to move on to the next stage—the stage of Creative Commitment.

STAGE FOUR: THE CREATIVE-COMMIT-MENT STAGE

This final stage develops out of the grounded recognition that what one has feared was only fear itself. Meeting new people evolves naturally out of the inner conviction that they offer a promise rather than a threat to one's way of life. The signal one sends out is: "Come closer at your own pace, for I would like to know you better. I will be comfortable with whatever consequences might or might not develop."

One tears up the shopping list in one's head: Each new person is seen as an individual in his or her own right and is given the time to express that individuality. One sees the expression of individuality as a two-way street where both you and the other person have an equal right to reveal yourselves at your own pace. Consequently, one guards against snap judgments after a first or second date about what a person is really like, or whether or not he or she is one's type. Since a relationship is not something that is "found," but is a development over time, one creates the time for a potential relationship to breathe. You don't have to come on too fast, or distance yourself. Because you are friendly with yourself, you can become friendly with others.

When the attraction exists, one allows new relationships to proceed at their own pace because one feels that living the relationship will determine its direction and possibilities rather than preconceived notions about how the relationship should or must develop. Since trust in oneself has developed, one's capacity to trust and evaluate others more realistically increases. One may sometimes remember the pain of other breakups as one becomes more intimately involved with a special person, but one recognizes the pain as a powerless echo from the past rather than as an accurate predictor of the breakup of the present relationship. Similarly, I-have-been-here-before feelings may flare up, but one is now in touch with the *differences* the new person possesses, though he or she may have superficial similarities to people one used to know.

In this stage, one does not view the ending of a relationship as a sign of failure or rejection, nor as an occasion to blame one's former partner. The hurt is felt but one does not wallow in self-pity. Instead, one tries to learn from the experience in order to improve the next relationship. A nonjudgmental evaluation of why this relationship went sour strengthens one's ability to trust oneself enough to risk a new relationship and act more perceptively next time. Though one still fears another mistake, one is confident that a new relationship will be an improvement over past relationships since it will incorporate one's growing awareness of what went wrong last time. No relationship is seen as meaningless, wasted, or failed. All relationships are viewed as stepping-stones toward an improved future.

When a new relationship grows in intimacy and seems to fit both parties (because it is based on friendship, caring, warmth, vulnerability, and love that includes growing mutual respect and trust as well as sexual delight), one feels the prospect of a monogamous commitment more as something to welcome than avoid. One will still have mixed feelings at this prospect, but the past that whispers escape-while-you-can has lost its pull. The knowledge that you are a different, more mature person today, and therefore capable of shaping a *new* outcome in a new relationship, overrides your fears and hesitations.

But one can clearly acknowledge the case against a monogamous commitment, such as a living-together arrangement or remarriage. The disruption of one's single-person life-style and the accommodation to a new interdependent life-style will heighten tensions; arguments, a clashing of interests, uncomfortable compromises may occur. One's freedom to act independently will be limited by the effect one's actions may have on the new partner. One will find that sexual adventures outside the new relationship will only destroy one's trust in each other.

However, the case for single life now sounds far less persuasive than it did when one was living through the previous stages of learning to love again. Wiser now, one can substitute realistic expectations for the pipe dream of believing that any one person can unconditionally satisfy *all* of one's needs. Abrasions occur when one lives with any person—even when one lives with oneself. A realization emerges that no sex is more exciting than sex combined with the love of a special person.

Functioning now as a whole person, instead of as the half-person one was in the first stage of learning to love again, one makes a commitment to a special person out of the need to belong *with* that person rather than *to* that person. One's fears of being swallowed up or victimized in the new relationship may surface again at the time of the commitment, but now one knows that those fears are based on what one *was* rather than what one *is* today. One's sensitivity, awareness, and self-assertion will prevent the past from repeating itself.

New forms in which close commitments can grow have arisen in our society in the past decade, including the living-together arrangement. When they have arrived at the creative commitment stage, many people today are opting for this arrangement. Some do so in place of marriage, others as an experimental step toward marriage. Whatever the form, call it living together or marriage, one regards the content of the committed relationship as the most significant definer of the validity of the relationship and its duration. One is aware that the joint creation of an environment in which each partner is encouraged to be who he or she is without pretense or defensiveness is the best guarantee that the relationship will be a loving and lasting one. In addition, one sets no advance together-till-the-end-of-time requirement on the relationship: To the extent that one renews the relationship each day by being sensitive, alert, compassionate, and assertive about one's own and each other's needs and limits, the relationship will be enhanced and will continue. Otherwise it will wither. Today is the day the opportunities are there to be seized, not yesterday or tomorrow.

You will be ready for a creative commitment when you feel the risk of taking such a step is less to be feared than not taking that step. For there is no guarantee that such a commitment will result in increased happiness. If you go into such a relationship in the belief that the other person is there to "make you happy," you will have planted seeds of destruction at the start. If you opt for it in the conviction that you and your partner are in a relationship to create the happiness that only can be derived from two whole people sharing themselves, bright possibilities exist.

Usually a readiness for a creative commitment arises in the third or fourth year after a divorce, but it can happen earlier or later. However, careful self-scrutiny is advised if the need seems to arise in the first or second year: Is that need based on the yearnings felt by a half-person who wants to be taken care of rather than grow as a human being? Or is it indeed based on an internal connection with the eleven lifelines to learning to love again that you experienced in your divorce? If those eleven lifelines have not been experienced yet, caution may prove to be the better decision when a possible partner enters the scene. Half-persons fall in love with what they have been programmed since childhood to believe is love; whole persons in a creative commitment fall in love with other whole persons.

TRANSITION MOVEMENTS BETWEEN STAGES

You may find yourself experiencing what Sue, thirty-four, and divorced three years ago, is concerned about: "It's like I'm in nowhere," Sue said. "Most of the time I'm in Stage Three, but other times I go back to Stage One or Two and then come back to Stage Three again. I don't feel good in anything I'm doing. What does that mean?"

Sue is experiencing a typical sign of progress in learning to love again, which she interpreted as a backward step. Moving back and forth between stages can be an indication that one feels self-confined in a given stage and finds the situation increasingly unsatisfactory. Sue was living mostly in the third stage, but occasionally retrogressed to the second or first stage. However, this was not a sign she was moving backward. On the contrary, it was an indication of a push within herself to move forward. Sue was dissatisfied with the stage she was in and wished to move to Stage Four but was confused, as well as fearful, about how to progress. In trying to solve her dilemma, she relied on what she already knew to try to relieve her discomfort. What she knew were the previous stages which once afforded her some satisfaction, and she thought they might again. But she had outgrown the previous stages and could never find the comfort she hoped to rediscover in them. Sue experienced the consequences of her dilemma as confusion and intense discomfort. But that very discomfort indicated she was ready to consciously reevaluate her wants and needs in relationships with the opposite sex. Her wants and needs had changed and now she was ready for the next stage forward which could accommodate her new outlook. This new outlook expressed itself in her readiness to move toward a creative commitment rather than remain self-confined in the selective-distancing stage. Sue could now direct her energies toward the future rather than the past, once she understood the real meaning of her movement back and forth between stages.

TIMING SENSITIVITY: MAKING RELATION-SHIPS GROW

Owen, thirty-six, divorced four years ago, recently shared the following experience with the other members of his LTLA group: "Eight months ago I met an attractive, intelligent woman. Anita was her name. We dated twice and I never called her again. I wish I had been aware then of the four stages of learning to love again because I think we could have had a great relationship. But she had been divorced only ten months previously and was boring me to death about what a rat her ex-husband was and about all of the new problems she was facing. Even so, there was something warm and charming about her; I suppose that's why I dated her a second time. But the garbage she dumped on me was too much and I never called her or saw her again. I'm kind of sad about that, because now I see I didn't understand where she was at or where I was at either. I thought then, well here we are two people, who are going to make it immediately—and if not good-bye.

"I didn't realize at that time that she was in a temporary place, that maybe she wouldn't have all of those hang-ups three months or six months later. I can see now that she was just coming out of that remembered-pain first stage you were talking about, Mel, and that I was in the selective-distancing third stage. Wow, I just realized that I was like Anita was during the first year of my own divorce. I feel sick when I think of how many women I must have turned off then. What I should have done was not end it like I did. It would have been better to have given Anita the space she needed to become a more secure person and not make any demands on her that she wasn't up to meeting then. I wanted her to pay attention only to me and love me right now; but she was into her own problems and had to get it together before anything like that could happen. I could have kept in touch with her on the phone and dated her occasionally even after that second date. But, I thought, if she's this way now, she will be this way forever. I don't think that's true any longer. After all, I changed, so I know other people change too. Come to think of it, maybe it's not all over yet. Maybe I'll call her up tomorrow and find out what she's like now."

Owen was finding out that his timing sensitivity could significantly affect the direction of a relationship. A lack of awareness of where the other person is at, and a lack of tolerance in allowing that person to proceed at his or her own pace, could end a relationship before it had the chance of flowering. Awareness and tolerance increases the chances for the blossoming of a relationship that might seem fragile at its beginning. There is every indication that Owen will put this knowledge to good use.

Owen's story pushed a memory button in my mind. It was so similar in some respects to my relationship with Pat, which I described in Chapter 1. The outcome was different, but it could easily have been the same. After all, when I met Pat, she was just emerging from her remembered-pain stage. Like Anita, she was in her first year of divorce. I, on the other hand, had just lived through the questing-experimental second stage and was beginning to want something more than just sex in a relationship. Our needs differed dramatically in many ways (Pat was still wearing her wedding ring; I was beyond the stage of reliving the past almost twenty-four hours a day). That disastrous first date of ours could easily have resulted in our not seeing each other again. However, we recognized we were at different stages in our development and did not let that fact end our relationship. Instead, we allowed each other to proceed at our own pace. Our relationship progressed on its own time schedule from a starting point of acquaintanceship, to friendship, and then to a sexual and love relationship in which our needs began to fully mesh. If either of us had demanded that a lasting love relationship had to happen now or never on our first, second, or third date, we would have prevented it from ever happening at all. A lasting love relationship doesn't happen overnight; in our case, the foundation took three years to build.

You can develop your timing sensitivity by alerting yourself to the reality that in any new relationship you may be at one stage, the other person at another. Don't consider that possibility to be a barrier to the further development of a relationship. If something worthwhile is present, acknowledge and tolerate the different stages of learning to love again each of you may be in. It may make the difference between another quick ending or a vital new beginning.

TURNING "YES-BUTS" INTO FRESH STARTS

The process of learning to love again is really the process of your growth beyond your divorce experience. That experience has given you new ground to stand on for taking more effective charge of your life. But it is only the takeoff point for learning to love again. Whether or not you indeed create the conditions for meeting a "special person" and enter into a creative commitment will depend on the way you live through each of the four stages outlined above. You must recognize that the stages do exist, understand the stage you are in at this time in your life, and act on your readiness feelings to move to the next stage. Each new stage is an improvement over the previous stage—a step forward in learning to love again.

However, the possibility of confining yourself in any one stage is very real. The kind of Yes-But complaints you repeatedly voice now are clues to the kind of self-confinement you may be experiencing. There are two kinds of self-confinement: One kind acts as a protective coating that serves the positive function of preventing you from progressing to the next stage of learning to love again before you are ready for that stage. The other tells you that you are ready for the next stage in learning to love again but don't know quite how to move into that stage

Lucy, a woman in her mid-thirties, typifies both kinds of self-confinement in the first, remembered-pain, stage. For the first four years after she divorced her alcoholic husband, Harry, after eleven years of marriage, she remained locked into a pattern that did not allow her to reach out for new relationships. She had to rid herself of a violent husband in a time-consuming two-year legal case; she had to care for two pre-teen-age daughters; she had to attend to her mother who was dying of cancer; and she had to upgrade her skills as an accountant and find self-supporting work. Creating a new stability in her life during the first three years after her divorce was her most pressing priority. "In the beginning it was like I was almost out of my mind. If I could survive one day at a time it felt like a victory," Lucy later told me. "Two years after I left Harry, my mother died and that tore me apart. My kids and I now get along well, but in the beginning it was pandemonium. And it took me a year and a half to get the accounting job I now have.

"It was true even then, I got very horny at times. After all, I'm a woman and I enjoy sex. Harry's drinking had made him practically impotent in the last three years of our marriage, so I felt very deprived and had all sorts of wild sex fantasies. I started to masturbate to relieve the tension, which was okay for a while but was really a second-best kind of thing. Sometimes I felt I should be going out and meeting new men, but I guess I was too scared of being hurt again. I always used the excuse, when one of my girl friends asked me to go out, that it was impossible to do so. I said I didn't have the time, my kids and my mother came first, and besides I couldn't find any baby-sitters and they were too expensive anyway."

At that time in her life, Lucy's Yes-Buts protected her from moving too fast too soon out of the remembered-pain stage. She needed the opportunity to develop greater confidence in her ability to solve the more immediate problems in her life before she could break through her cocoon. That breakthrough occurred in the fourth year after her divorce. By then she had established a stable life but continued to use the same Yes-Buts whenever a woman friend would ask her to a singles organization: "I kept on using the argument that there were no baby-sitters that could be trusted, besides there were none around—and, oh yes, I was always too tired to go out," Lucy reflected. "But then a funny thing happened that made me change. For the first time in years, I felt a sudden urge to window-shop dresses in some of my favorite stores. I didn't expect to buy anything, but suddenly I saw a very dressy dress and said that's for me. It was so unlike my other dresses—a bright Kelly-green chiffon gown; all my old clothes were kind of drab grays and beige and black. I felt kind of guilty about spending the money on myself, but I must say I enjoyed it. I even said to myself then that someday I might be able to wear it at a party, although I hadn't been to a party in years. Well, it wasn't more than a week after I bought the dress that my friend Joyce asked me to go out to a singles dance. As soon as she asked me I began to use the same old excuses against going out. But Joyce said she had been involved in a co-op baby-sitting arrangement for the last year that didn't cost anything but the time she donated in exchange, and that the sitters were all responsible grown-ups like ourselves. Do you know it was like she was telling me this for the first time, but as a matter of fact she had told me this a dozen times before but I never really listened to her. Or if I did, I used the excuse of being too tired. But this time I said to myself, why not go out and wear that dress? Something must have been brewing inside me for quite some time before Joyce asked. I remember getting more and more bored and dissatisfied with myself and my broken-record excuses for not going out months before Joyce made her suggestion. I guess I was ready to take a chance. So with Joyce's help I did make the arrangements to go out and have been going out ever since.''

What Lucy learned was that for the first three years after her divorce her Yes-Buts protected her from dissipating her energies so that she could concentrate on the situations in her life that were crying for attention. But in the fourth year the same Yes-Buts became triggers for positive change: The more she became bored with her own excuses, the more she demonstrated a readiness to move out of her remembered-pain stage. She had already laid the groundwork that enabled her to reach out to new relationships by creating stability in her life. Even though the new relationships might be shallow in the second stage, they would be a positive step toward meeting and exposing herself to new people and satisfying her very human needs. In the second stage she might learn that the realities of promiscuous sex differed from her illusions of sex as salvation and that she was perhaps readying herself for the third stage of learning to love again, the selective-distancing stage.

It would have been inappropriate for Lucy to move out of her first stage in less than four years just because well-meaning people insisted she do so. Just like every other divorced person, Lucy had to move at her own pace; four years were uniquely right for her. Readiness time for a new stage cannot be forced or determined externally. Lucy was ready to take Joyce's well-meaning suggestions at a particular time but not earlier. You too will progress when the time is right for you. Your own feelings are the best guidelines for appropriate action.

What are those feelings that indicate your readiness to take a new look at your situation? Surprisingly enough, they are the very feelings most of us have been taught in our culture to fear and avoid: boredom, discomfort, dissatisfaction, anxiety, turbulence, confusion, frustration, anger, despair. Instead of trying to deny, ignore, or run from these feelings which you may be mislabeling as "negative" or "bad," now is the time for owning up to them and understanding the positive implications they hold for your life. It is time to remember what you may have forgotten: You did exactly that in your divorce experience in order to understand the creative meaning your emotional turmoil held for you at that time in your life. The enemy is not these mislabeled negative feelings, but the supposedly "positive" feeling of complacency. Complacency offers us the security of settling for what we already have at the expense of improving the quality of our lives. Improvement requires risk-taking. To nurture complacency is to stop moving toward a creative commitment. Lucy herself indicated how her dissatisfaction made her take a step forward. She also had what I call an attack of "the suddenlies." As she said, she "suddenly" felt the urge to window-shop new dresses. This is another kind of positive clue. "Suddenly" doesn't happen suddenly in any person. When you hear yourself saying you suddenly thought or did something which seems foreign to your character, it means forces inside of yourself have been working a long time to point you in a new direction. Lucy's "suddenly" wanting a dress was a sign of her readiness to move into the questing-experimental stage of learning to love again. Her acceptance of Joyce's invitation to go out together was the way she translated that readiness into action. Had Lucy been complacent rather than dissatisfied, nothing would have happened. Complacency would have kept her confined in that first stage of remembered pain perhaps for many years to come.

Most not-so-recently divorced men and women probably are at present in the third stage, the selective-distancing stage, of learning to love again. The problems Lucy has faced are already behind them. They are confronting new obstacle courses. However, there are very many not-so-recently divorced people still locked into those earlier stages regardless of how many years they have been divorced. The large number of such people include at least as many men as women. The need for mature intimacy is not exclusive to one sex. We are all the same in our basic human desire to enhance the quality of our emotional lives.

Should you be like Lucy and find yourself locked in Stage One or Two, you can begin by recognizing that there are four stages to learning to love again, rather than a jungle of feelings you don't know how to begin to untangle. These stages are *learning experiences* you live through in order to improve the quality of your life. Trust your intelligence and feelings to derive the maximum knowledge about yourself and others as you live through each stage: You are no longer the vulnerable, loveless rejected child you may fear you are. Identify that fear as an I-have-been-here-before feeling that is not telling you anything real about yourself today; it is only a ghost of the past that you can exorcise if you are motivated to do so. There is nothing bad or good about the four stages of learning to love again other than what you make out of your experiences in each of these stages. The four stages are opportunities for reaching a creative commitment. However, you determine whether or not you will seize those opportunities or ignore their existence.

The recommendations I have made in the previous paragraph apply with even greater relevance to the thousands of men and women currently locked into the third stage, the selective-distancing stage of learning to love again. It is precisely because these men and women have already achieved so much in their knowledge of who they are and in their relationships with the opposite sex that they now feel at such a dead end! For these are the people that possess the greatest capabilities for engaging in a creative commitment: They have earned those capabilities in the process of living through the earlier stages of learning to love again. But because they are ready to establish the conditions for engaging in a creative commitment, they fear it the most. This is not so surprising a statement as it may seem. A man on a low rung of the corporation ladder wants to be appointed to a higher position, believes he can handle it, and fights like the devil to get it. But when he gets it, he will typically become anxious and depressed, and may even turn it down. Or a woman complains about her menial job because she knows she can do well in a better job. But when offered the possibility of training for the better job, she feels threatened and helpless, and turns it down. The capabilities of this man and woman are real, but their fear of failure defeats their own best interests.

This process is magnified ten-thousandfold in the third stage of learning to love again since choices affecting the most vulnerable part of yourself are being presented. Consequently, anxieties about possible failure and subsequent unhappiness block out the reality of your present capabilities and accomplishments. This self-imposed barrier against your readiness to create the conditions for a creative commitment is what I term "commitment anxiety."

Commitment anxiety is the breeding ground for Yes-Buts. The anxiety is *imagined* as a protective device that will guard you against future pain. It is more comfortable to accept your *present* discomfort if you believe that a love commitment will inevitably result in another painful breakup. Commitment anxiety intensifies as a love commitment appears more immediately possible. Kay, a woman divorced four years ago, looked very disturbed as she told me, "It's so strange, really. My relationship with Bob is getting stronger and stronger. I like him so much I'm ready to believe I love him. So I can't understand what happens to me when my ex-husband comes to my house to take our son out. Lately, when I see my ex I think how handsome he is and can't help comparing him to Bob. He's so much handsomer than Bob. He's such a super-dresser, while Bob always looks like he's come out of a dime store. My ex is making lots more money than Bob and he's so poised and self-assured. I know my ex hasn't changed the slightest inside—he's as arrogant and self-centered as ever, so I could never go back to him. But he seems more attractive to me now and I feel so angry with myself. It's like I'm being unfaithful to Bob when I think of my ex that way and it frightens me. Why is this happening to me now?"

Commitment anxiety can and does perform a positive as well as negative function if it alerts you to looking before you leap. It can give you the time to more accurately assess the reality of a relationship you may have many illusions about. But it can and does prevent a creative commitment if you allow it to flood every new relationship you experience.

Since you have already taken giant steps toward attaining a creative commitment, the third stage is the time for consolidating your gains. Now is the time to reflect on what you have learned from living through the first two stages of learning to love again. Now is the time to compare where you are and where you were in the remembered-pain stage. You are putting the cart before the horse if you are right now comparing where you are to where you would like to be. You have to find out how far you have traveled before you can determine how far you have to go. Let's take a look at what most men and women learn about themselves and others in these early stages:

1. *Overcoming earlier Yes-But obstacles.* In Stages One and Two, you complained you couldn't meet new people, you feared that nobody was available and that even if they were, they would reject you. The reality proved otherwise.

2. *Coping with rejection.* Being rejected didn't destroy you as you first thought it would. You learned that there were different strokes for different folks. Not fitting another person's ideal did not mean you were "bad" or "worthless." A typical comment I have heard from many men and women is, "If somebody rejects me it probably has something to do with that person, not me. After all how

could that person really know what I'm like after
only a five-minute conversation or one date?''

3. *Finding out that taking the risk of being rejected
   usually has a positive payoff.* As one woman said,
   "If I see a man I might find attractive at a party and
   he's looking at me, I will go over and introduce
   myself, even though I'm a little scared. That's just
   normal to be kind of anxious, but I don't let it stop
   me. I figure that if I meet him and the conversation
   and his personality doesn't turn me on, or I don't
   turn him on, the world isn't going to end tomorrow. On the other hand, it might be the beginning
   of something pleasant—and more often than not it
   is.''

4. *Discovering you are more than you think you are.*
   You've learned to surprise yourself by asserting
   yourself in ways you never thought possible even
   two or three years ago. You found you could initiate new relationships or involve yourself in new
   hobbies or work. You proved you could grow and
   change for the better without using your age as an
   excuse for staying home and doing nothing. The
   process of melting your frozen love-image has
   already begun.

5. *Learning to set your own limits and horizons.* What
   suits you rather than what suits other people is
   more and more a determining factor in your life.
   As one man told me, "I'm giving myself space
   now and don't feel I have to be a man-about-town
   to preserve my image as a sexy guy. During the
   first two years after my divorce I was very shy and

afraid of rejection. I just sat in front of my television set and lived mainly for my children's visits. After that I really tore up the town and tried to make every woman I met. Now I'm into reading some novels I always wanted to read but never had time for, and it feels good.''

6. *Building up a trust and liking for yourself.* You have found it is no longer intolerable to be alone with yourself. You enjoy doing nice things for yourself, like playing records or reading. You have begun to trust your ability to improve the quality of your life. You have learned you can make new friends and have developed a trust in your ability to do so.

To sum up: You have changed—and unless you recognize that you are far better able to cope with the challenges of attaining a lasting love relationship *today* than you were before, you may end up confining yourself to the third stage.

THE CHANGED YOU AND TURNABOUT THINKING

The apparent dead ends you face in the third stage are markedly different from those in the earlier stages. You no longer hear yourself complaining that you can't leave home to go out and meet people, that you can't find men or women who will like you. You have already met a sizable number of people, so now your complaints are about the quality—or lack of quality—of your new relationships. The Yes-But complaints now become: "I can't find a meaningful relationship; every person I date I see only once or twice because there's nothing there; I'm always making mistakes; there are no interesting people; every heavy relationship I get into breaks up after two or three months, which proves I can't trust anyone; I've tried going everywhere but all the people I come in contact with are dull and superficial; there are no people my age that are appealing; there is a shortage of attractive single men in my town. . . ." As long as you continue to think, feel, and act as you are currently doing, you will continue to race around the locked room of your frustrations. Now is the time for you to get in touch with the competencies you have already built up inside yourself and use those competencies to reevaluate your situation in a more realistically hopeful light. You already have established the preconditions for re-examination. The key to unlocking the door of that frustration room is in your hand: It is Turnabout Thinking.

Turnabout Thinking is a tool you can apply to situations that appear to be dead ends. Instead of making your usual response to a problem, turn the problem about and look at it from a different point of view. Solutions you never thought possible may turn up. Turnabout Thinking isn't foreign to your experience. You used it when you turned your divorce into a creative experience. Instead of continuing to be devastated by your divorce (as you probably were during the early months), a time came when you began to feel differently: You began to see your divorce as an opportunity for growth. When that happened, new solutions to the problems you had thought insurmountable became possible. In the third stage of learning to love again, apply Turnabout Thinking to your present difficulties. Here is how it can be applied:

Instead of reacting to unsatisfying relationships as "mistakes" you have made, turnabout and see them as learning experiences.

If you continue to mislabel every relationship as a mistake, a new relationship will become another "mistake." You will continue to send out signals to the opposite sex that you are fearful and hesitant of making another error; and your fear will pervade any new relationship. Your inability to trust yourself to make a "right" decision will automatically result in your distancing a new person at the very start, and you will wind up confirming your judgment that you always make "mistakes."

A turnabout understanding of your "failed" relationships may produce the kind of positive results that Beverly, thirty-two, an outgoing woman in one of my LTLA groups, recently experienced. Beverly came to one of the sessions feeling crushed. "Tod left me five days ago and I feel like dying," she said tearfully. "It was the longest relationship I had had with anyone in the five years since my divorce—one whole year—and it's all turned into nothing. I'm still trying to figure it out. We had this huge fight and then I didn't hear from him for four days. I should have suspected something was up when that happened, because he used to at least phone every day and spend weekends with me. That was the last time I saw him; all he did was call up to say it was over because he no longer could stand my arguments all the time. 'Since I'm such an irritant in your life, I don't want to cause you any more distress,' was the way he put it. He was such a great guy. When I met him I had been out of work and he supported me for a while. He was like a knight on a white horse the way he got me my job with the insurance company and how he was able to get my landlord to make the plumbing repairs that I could never get done on my own. He's a take-charge guy and so personable and I'm sorry that I lost him. There was an awful lot of nice cozy physical stuff in our relationship. Maybe it would have been different if I never showed my anger. I got the picture from him a long time ago that I shouldn't show anger. 'Why can't you ever agree with me?' he used to say. He would call all of my opinions stupid.''

It turned out that Beverly's pain and anguish were only the tip of the iceberg. Her dissatisfaction with the relationship had been brewing for months. The huge fight that was the superficial cause of the breakup really was an expression of the fundamentally different values Beverly and Tod held about people and the environment. ''The argument was over an ecology issue in the next election,'' Beverly continued. ''I said the land had to be protected, and he was saying the land should be raped. But that was Tod, a land speculator. He hated most of my friends, who are artists and musicians. Bleeding hearts he called them. He used to get furious when I stood up for them. I'd go to those business cocktail parties and he and his buddies would stand there and talk about how they just cut up their competition into little pieces and how the war in Vietnam could have been won by dropping a nuclear bomb. Horrible!''

So what appeared to be Tod's rejection of Beverly also turned out to be Beverly's rejection of Tod. Beverly herself had set the stage for rejecting Tod by defending her friends and her different political views, knowing this would irritate him. She operated out of mixed feelings but was really ready to do the leaving herself because she found she liked being assertive and no longer felt the need to be taken care of if that meant the destruction of her own individuality. When this was brought to Beverly's attention, she no longer saw the relationship as a failure and its loss as a tragedy. The end of the relationship signified Beverly's readiness to move toward a more fulfilling relationship that would incorporate what she learned about herself and men from the experience with Tod. She had learned that while she still liked a take-charge kind of guy who was personable and sexy, other qualities, such as mutual respect, tenderness, sensitivity, and a similar set of values were equally important. In the future she would not be so easily attracted to another strong man who would nurture her only if she relinquished her personhood.

I heard from Beverly later and this is what she told me: "Would you believe it, around three weeks after Tod left I met a guy and after I dated him for a month he asked me to move in with him. I was tempted. I'm kind of disorganized at running my live—I always feel there's someone who can do it better for me. Once I would have jumped at the chance, but not after my experience with Tod. So I turned him down— after all he didn't really know what I'm like any more than I did him. He was another wealthy businessman and his attitudes were like Tod's. That gave me warning enough to look before I leap.

"After that I had three short-term relationships. I don't look at them as failures just because they've ended. All three men had something nice to offer me to which I could respond. With the first it was strictly an erotic thing. He really helped me get in touch with my own sexuality in more exciting ways than anyone else ever did. I learned I'm a sexier person than I thought I was. The next guy was a real buddy-buddy. He listens to me and respects what I have to say, even when he disagrees. I learned from him that you could be friendly with a man, just friendly like a brother, without sex. If somebody told me that a year ago I would have said that would be impossible. The third guy was just a spontaneous fun person. He helped me learn to laugh again and made me realize how much I value a plain fun-to-be-with person who does things at times on the spur of the moment, a guy who isn't uptight all the time. They were all rewarding experiences. It was like a different side of me came out in each relationship.

"I think I know better now what I want in a good relationship—a mix of all these qualities I experienced in the men I've gone out with. One thing is certain—I'm not going overboard any more and believe a guy is the one true love of my life just because he has one or two qualities that turn me on. I've got to find out whether or not he has those other qualities I value also. And, you know, I feel it in my bones that it's going to happen, the guy with the right mix for me. I don't know when, but sometime when I'm not expecting it, probably, it will happen."

It may have happened six months later when Beverly met Spencer on a Sierra Club hike. "I look terrible when I'm hiking," she told me recently. "My hair gets frizzy and I get all wet with perspiration. But Spencer said he was attracted to my personality immediately when we met. He's an artist in a small advertising agency and there are so many nice things about him. He really digs my assertiveness. But I'm taking this relationship one step at a time. None of that let's go to bed first and then get acquainted stuff I used to fall for. I get nice warm feelings with him, but I'm not putting a label like instant love on them like I used to. I'll see what happens without pushing."

What Beverly is doing is applying turnabout thinking in her life and as a result is learning from her past experiences instead of repeating them. Her discoveries about herself and how she was relating to men are not exceptional—more and more people are coming to the same realization she has arrived at. That realization (which applies equally to men) was best summarized by a forty-two-year-old woman who said in an LTLA group: "I met a friend the other day who said, 'Joan, you had so many affairs and you look great!' I told her things aren't always great but that I never made any mistakes. She was surprised and said that I must be crazy because everyone makes mistakes. I explained that I don't believe that's true. I have learned millions of lessons, but I have never made a mistake. It may have seemed at the time like a stupid thing to do. But I don't consider that a mistake, because I learned not to get myself into the same box again in exactly that same way. And that alone is saying a lot. I no longer get into relationships where I walk in blindly over and over again. I've learned to stop, look, and understand."

Instead of claiming interesting people are simply not available, turnabout and consider that you may be limiting your possibilities for finding them.

Are you giving the other person equal time to fully express himself or herself when you go out on a date before you conclude your evening has been a waste of time? You may have been with interesting people without even knowing it if you find yourself always ending a relationship after a first, second, or third date. One man who learned that he was doing this told me how he changed: "It takes time to know another person. It dawned on me that I would be pissed-off if somebody made a snap judgment about what kind of person I am after a first or second date and then never saw me again. And I bet that's what some of the people I took out were doing to me just like I did it to others! Now, I don't expect the impossible. On a first or second date you can only go just so far. It's a beginning, and a beginning is always awkward with a lot of phony role-playing. I don't pour my whole life story out any more like I used to. My God, how I used to talk and talk and not listen. Now I just present what I really feel—that here's a chance to show my genuine interest in getting to know another person a little better; to listen to what that person has to say instead of always being so self-conscious of how I was coming across. It works, too. It's only after the first three dates that the masks start slipping off, and you find there's a person underneath who is more interesting than you expected. In the past I would have prevented myself from meeting that person. Come to think of it, a relationship of any kind really begins at the fourth date. Before that time the garbage has to be cleared away.''

Are your expectations creating your failed hopes? If you go to a singles organization affair, discussion group, dance, or a bar convinced that you *must* meet and get a date with someone interesting or you will have ''failed,'' you will be guaranteeing your ''failure.'' For you have already learned by your past experience to expect ''failure'' and you bring your expectations to each new situation. As one man told me, ''I program myself when I go out. I go to five different singles organizations and give myself one half hour in each place to find an interesting person. And when I don't and the half hour is up I split to the next place. I've been doing this for a year and it's kind of getting like Mission Impossible. I feel lousy when I don't find somebody I can take home. Like being a loser—other people make out, why can't I?''

Another man who has attended many singles organizations shared this relevant observation:

"Men and women both are always so apologetic when they come to a singles group, as if it's wrong for them to be there. A man will say to a woman, 'I've never been here before,' or 'I came here six months ago,' even though he's pretty much of a regular. Or a woman will say in answer to 'Why do you come here?' 'Oh, I don't know, I just like to come here' instead of acknowledging the normal desire she has to meet new men. What she shows is her fear of meeting new people even though she wants to meet new people. Because there's a social hour after a lecture and most of these women split immediately for home like frightened deer, instead of socializing with the men. And those are the women who complain the most about the lack of interesting men in their lives! There are guys in singles organizations who are really mellow—and not every guy in a high-class singles bar is a bum either. But we men need the chance to show ourselves as nice people, instead of getting a panicky reaction from the women. For example, the few women who stick around for the social hour are usually so uptight it's like trying to penetrate a wall. They stand around waiting for the men to take the first step in introducing themselves. I think most women are still hung up on males being the doers and females being the receivers. I'm not saying the men at these singles groups are any better. Most of them feel they are pretty much losers for having to stoop to a singles organization to meet people. It's like a threat to their image of themselves as being strong men. And while the women stand around waiting for men to approach them during the social hour, the men are sweating and staring and scared half to death that they will be rejected if they even so much as say hello to a woman who catches their eye! As I see it, if you go to a singles group thinking you are a loser and that everyone else there is a loser (because you think of a singles organization as a dumping ground for rejects), your suspicions will be confirmed. If you feel like a loser, you will be a loser.''

Organizations like singles clubs, dating services, and high-class singles bars are neither good nor bad. They are simply opportunities for socializing and meeting people. What you do with these opportunities is up to you. Your expectations, and the degree to which you feel comfortable in allowing new people to enter your life, will determine whether or not you will meet interesting people in those environments.

I asked Elaine, a woman in her mid-thirties who was puzzled about women's complaints that they can't seem to meet interesting men, why she was puzzled. She replied, ''It's like this. I'm an outgoing person and always meet people wherever I go. I've met lots of women who've become wonderful friends, as well as men. I don't go out to find or meet men. I go to places and events that interest me. Most of the interesting men I've met are doing things that interest me, and they show up at the places I go to. Like I took a night course at a community college in oil painting and sure enough I met a guy there who has since become a good friend of mine. That happens all the time. I like going to conferences and one-day workshops that deal with political issues and the men who are attracted to me and me to them are there. If I don't meet a man at any of these places I like to go to, it's no big deal or tragedy. After all, I haven't lost anything. At the very least I went to a place I wanted to go to; I learned something new and that always feels great. And if I meet a man at those places, it's like the cherry on the cake—but I

already got the cake. Sometimes I've met nice men at the
cheese counter in the supermarket or in the elevator of the
building in which I work. I'll start the conversation if I'm
attracted. Not in any pushy manner. It's not what I say—that
can be as little as 'Hello, I see you like Cheddar cheese.
That's one of my favorites too.' It's the fact that I show him
I'm a friendly person who might like to know him a little bit
better.

"I'm on a lot of mailing lists, too, because everywhere I
go I usually sign up. Some time ago I went to a lecture at the
Unitarian Church on male and female sexuality, and oh was
that interesting. I put my name down on the mailing list and
the next thing that happened was that I started getting a lot of
mailings about a lot of other things I never knew existed
before. Like conferences on managing your money and on
the meaning of dreams and fantasies. They sounded kind of
intriguing, so I said why not and went to some of them. I've
expanded my interests as a result. Of course I've met some
fascinating men at these conferences also. They happened to
be there just like I happened to be there."

*Instead of always falling into dead-end relationships,
turnabout and regard your increasing dissatisfaction with
what seems to repeatedly happen as a sign of your readiness to act in new ways that will produce more satisfying
results.*

When you change your reasons for going to a lecture, an
outdoor club hike, or a singles party, you will be presenting
yourself differently and will change your way of acting
toward other people. In turn, more interesting people will be
attracted to you. Dan, a forty-five-year-old man divorced
five years ago, makes this observation:

"I used to go to all the singles clubs and hate myself for having to go there. I saw everyone there as if they were merchandise on display, waiting to be picked up or ignored, me included. After a long time, I got the message that nobody was there just because they enjoyed the chance of socializing with people, and if something happens, okay, and if not, okay, too. Everybody thought they had to make out, and if they didn't, it would be the end of the world. One night I walked home alone from a singles club and was very sore at not having scored. Why couldn't some of those more attractive women I was giving the eye see what an intelligent, sensitive, fun kind of guy I am? I put the blame on them; the stupid broads is what I thought. And then it suddenly dawned on me when I got home that night that I had been acting the same way those women were acting! They were tense, uptight, aloof, and afraid of being rejected like I was. All we were showing each other was that we were scared bunnies. How could they see the real me when I was presenting a false front of believing I was coming across like a suave man about town. When I was giving them the eye I thought, 'Come and get me, ladies, I'm a prize.' But they must have thought of me as a stuck-up guy who was threatening to them!

"The next time I went to that singles club I made a point to see if what I had suddenly realized was right. I didn't go to score, but to observe. Sure enough, I had hit the target. I changed after that, sort of acted more natural. I began to get acquainted with more women at those clubs by being more at ease with myself. That helped me to make the women I approached more at ease too, so we could have some pleasant conversation instead of grunts and come up and see my etchings talk. It seemed that the way I was presenting myself had an effect on the way they were reacting toward me. It sounds stupid, but I never thought of it that way before. I was so into myself at those singles affairs that I never thought of the other people there as being simply people. Not objects to be grabbed or Frankenstein monsters if they turned down my passes, just people like myself. Once I realized all of this, another thing happened. I found out that the very same women I was calling stupid broads without even meeting them were very interesting, intelligent people. Not all of them, of course, but far more than I ever dreamed of. All they needed was a chance to show what they really were like. And when I gave them that chance, they also gave me the same chance to show who I really was.

"However, I don't go to these single clubs as often as I used to any more. It's not because I can't meet interesting people there; it's because it's usually too heavy a scene. Too many people have protective shells around them that they refuse to open. It's like they *want* to feel rejected, strange as that seems. I don't want to spend all my energy all the time trying to get to know people better who don't want you to get to know them better. So now I've broadened my interests and I go to lots of other places where I meet people. I now date women who have never been married and widows too. I don't limit myself any longer to dating divorced women. I once thought divorced people could only date other divorced people. That sounds so weird to me now. Now I just go out with people period. I don't put labels on them in advance."

Dan's point about labeling others also applies to the way we may be labeling ourselves. Our self-labeling often freezes us into acting in ways that limit our chances for a lasting love relationship. If you say you like to go out only with certain kinds of people, or to take part only in certain kinds of activities, you may be missing the chance to meet interesting people—who may not necessarily match your labels, but who may very well match your basic need to love and be loved.

If you are becoming more and more dissatisfied with the feeling that you are meeting only the same kind of people, the time has arrived to tear up your self-labels. When Nicole, a thirty-two-year-old woman divorced three years ago after an eight-year marriage, tore up her self-labels, this is what happened:

"I'm falling deeply in love with David and it's a mind-blower for me. This man is beautiful inside, but when I first met him on the tennis court in the singles complex where I live, my first impression was that he was not my type. When he asked me out for dinner, my first reaction was to say no, thank you. I'm the kind of person who used to say before I met David that I could only go out with men slightly older than myself, who were six feet tall (I'm five-foot-seven). They had to have dark hair and be slim. David was none of these—he's four years younger than I am, he's only five feet eight, and he has blond hair and a slight paunch. So I started making excuses like I worked and had a five-year-old daughter to take care of. But he was very determined to go out and there was something about the way he smiled that attracted me, so I said okay in spite of myself. When he picked me up for dinner my heart sank. I've always been turned on by men who wear well-designed clothes—I'm a clotheshorse myself. But there was David at the door dressed in a jacket and pants that must have been high style in the fifties. There goes my nine dollars in baby-sitting expenses down the drain, I thought. But the evening turned out to be very nice. I found David so interesting to talk to and felt so comfortable with him that nothing else mattered. He wasn't the highly successful business type that I thought I could only like. He was a chemist who worked for Standard Oil, wrote poetry, and loved the outdoors like I did. As I got to know him better, I found out he was a creative, bright, intelligent, warm, sensitive, caring kind of person. All of the qualities I least expected to find in a person like him. And those qualities have always been most important to me. But I used to think they could only be attached to tall, dark, handsome, wealthy men. Of course they never were, but I always used to hope. Now that outside front no longer matters. But I did say to David the other night, 'I love you, David, but there's one thing going against you—you are a rotten dresser.' He looked at me with a funny look and said, 'I don't spend on clothes what you spend on clothes.' I told him it was not what he was spending but what he was choosing. So we've reached an agreement that the next time he buys an outfit I'll go with him and make suggestions that he can take or turn down. We can be open with each other and it feels so good. I told my friend Shana that my relationship with David is like good wine—I want to sip it and enjoy it. Shana reminded me that I once told her I would never date anyone younger than myself, or who wasn't tall. I said that was true, but that now I'll never say, 'You're not my type of person or I'm not your type of person' again.''

In contrast to Nicole, there was Lewis, the type of person who labeled himself "the funny guy." He had believed that women would like him only because he could crack jokes. An incident in his LTLA group helped him to tear up that label. He was saying, "Ever since my high school days I've had to have other things to make up for a lack of my being physically attractive. For instance, I had to become captain of the track team and president of my graduating class to get desirable women. Most of all I have a good sense of humor and that's why women are attracted to me. But they never stick around long.''

Before Lewis could speak any further, two women interrupted him. One of them said, ''Lewis, I think you are physically quite attractive, how could you think otherwise?'' Another said, ''But you're handsome! I don't know why you think your wisecracks and show biz act turn women on. Sure you're an amusing person, but when you are on-stage all the time like you are it gets mighty boring. If you could relax and just be yourself, you'd come on so much more sexy and attractive.''

Lewis learned that people saw him differently than he saw himself. He began to change from ''the funny man'' to a man who felt comfortable in his own skin and could radiate his sense of personal security to others. Instead of trying too hard and winding up with one-night stands, he began to meet people who were receptive to in-depth relationships.

ADVICE FROM THE FIRING LINE

I recently asked Barbara Hana Austin, the director of Executive Singles Directory, a personalized dating service in San Francisco, what she considers the most helpful advice for people who want a lasting love relationship. Barbara, a divorced mother, is a warm, expressive woman in her forties who has counseled thousands of men and women. Because her comments are so meaningful and relevant, I would like to share them with you now:

''I really care for people, that's why I established my service,'' Barbara said. ''The people who like who they are and what they are are the ones who have their relationships work out. They don't have those two faces most people have—the one face they show to others and the face they show to themselves. They are their own people. They are who they are all of the time. There's no fake front, and they are not afraid to say 'I'd like to get to know who you are and what you are feeling.' They are the people who are outward with their feelings and listen to the other person too. Even shy people can open up to another person. It may be difficult the first time, but it gets easier and easier and they learn that it produces positive results.

"You have to trust yourself before you can trust anyone else. If you don't have fear, or don't allow the fear to prevent you from taking a chance, you will trust. Anyone who is manipulated and has not learned from what has happened deserves to be manipulated. You protect yourself from being manipulated by showing that you are a person who is secure in yourself. People who are manipulators steer clear of persons like that.

"Fear destroys relationships. Don't let the fear stop you from jumping into whatever is here right now as an opportunity. It's okay to tell the other person that you are a little anxious or uncertain if you do the approaching, that only makes you more human. The other person knows what you are feeling because he or she is feeling the same thing. So long as you basically like yourself, everything will turn out okay. You can't expect others to give you the trust and security that you may think you lack. You have to give that to yourself."

5 The Living-Together Arrangement: A Testing Ground for Learning to Love Again

The current prevalence of living-together arrangements is a measure of our society's changing attitudes. Less than ten years ago, living together without benefit of clergy was considered immoral. Today, the LTA (as the living-together arrangement has become known) is a fact of American life that is tabulated by the United States Census Bureau; in the past decade, the Census Bureau reports that LTA's have more than doubled. Almost one and a half million unmarried men and women acknowledge living together. Quite likely this is a gross underestimation of the actual number, since many more people practice the same arrangement quietly and do not appear in statistical tabulations.

LTA's exist throughout the country, whether they are acknowledged openly or kept private. National magazines, newspapers, films, television and radio programs objectively report on this new phenomenon as a reality of American life. The people who live together are not freaks but moral, decent, normal people.

Most unmarried men and women currently living together have been married before. (Pat and I were part of this group for almost a year before we married.) They range in age from the middle twenties to the sixties. Ten years ago, the small number of LTA's were unmarried college students in their late teens or early twenties. Rather than considering this a sign that the young have corrupted older men and women, I have come to believe this new trend is moral. Lynn, a forty-one-year-old registered nurse, divorced five years ago, affirms the change in attitude that many not-so-recently-divorced men and women have experienced: "A week ago," Lynn said, "my nineteen-year-old son, Terry, told me he was going to marry his girl friend, Donna. If that had happened ten years ago I would have been very pleased and would have given him my blessing. Instead, I started to question him about how long he had been going with Donna and what he knew about her and was he prepared to assume new responsibilities as a husband. It turned out he hardly knew the girl. He had dated her about twice a week for the past three months. She had no skills and the job he had as an insurance clerk could hardly support the two of them. It seemed to me that he was setting the stage for a divorce rather than a marriage, but his standard answer to everything I said was: 'But, Mom, we love each other!' I then suggested that he and Donna live together before they get married to get to know more about each other, even though they were madly in love. I wanted Terry to experience what it is really like living with another person twenty-four hours a day before he made such an important decision. Would you believe it, Terry was shocked! He said, 'Why Mom, I'm surprised at you—you of all people to suggest something like that!'

"Terry's remark sort of stunned me for a moment. I suppose I was as surprised at what I said as Terry was. Even two years ago I thought living-together arrangements were something 'bad' people did. I come from a religious background and take my religion seriously. But the more I thought about what I had said to Terry, the more I felt I was right. After all, is it more moral to marry someone you know practically nothing about and then be disappointed? Is it fair to the person you are marrying—or to yourself for that matter—not to know in advance what the pressures and responsibilities of marriage are like and then run away from the marriage when things get too tough? Is it more moral to marry like I did, without knowing a darn thing about myself or my husband sexually or otherwise? Just that he looked handsome in his naval uniform and that we liked each other's company in the four months we knew each other on dates. And for that both he and I paid the penalty of a marriage of seventeen years both of us were not suited for. As I look back on my own marriage, I can see now that the most moral thing that could have happened was to have lived together before our marriage. It probably would have meant we never would have married in the first place. But wouldn't that have been better than two decent people (which we both were) torturing each other for so many years? I can see now that the height of immorality is to deceive yourself and each other about the person you really are. If living together before marriage can correct that, then to me that is something to praise rather than to put down. I intend to marry again, but before I do, I know I would have to live with that person beforehand.''

Lynn has recognized that the living-together arrangement is an option available to people today. It is neither good nor bad in itself. It can, however, be used as a morally based learning experience if you are ready to use it as such. Each person must decide the morality question for himself or herself. When Pat and I agreed to enter into a living-together arrangement, we had to determine for ourselves this very issue. We recognized that some people might look askance at our arrangement, but we had to ask ourselves whether our morals were determined by other people's opinions or by what we felt was right for ourselves. Our upbringings differed little from Lynn's and we felt the same way that Lynn did about the morality of living together unmarried. We subsequently found that our living-together arrangement was an intermediate stage in our learning to love again. It proved to be a bridge between the selective-distancing stage, which Pat and I were in at the time we decided to live together, and the creative-commitment stage of our marriage one year later.

More and more not-so-recently divorced men and women who wish to test their readiness for a creative commitment choose to enter into a living-together arrangement, just as Pat and I did. For those persons who wish to experience daily intimacy with a special person, but who still believe such intimacy might repeat their marital history, the LTA is a useful testing ground to discover whether the past "must" be repeated. It is also a laboratory in which new ways of relating can be put into practice. Most important, it can provide the permissive kind of atmosphere needed to help you find what you truly want for yourself at this time in your life. It can enable you to separate out your mixed feelings, your illusions and fantasies, and come to terms with what suits you. An LTA experience can widen your awareness of yourself and your partner as two unique human beings, so that no matter whether you continue the relationship, marry, or break it up, the experience will have proved valuable. You may surprise yourself—as many LTAers have done—by finding out that you were not ready for a creative commitment, or that you prefer to remain unmarried, or that staying in the selective-distancing stage suits you, or that you don't want to modify your life-style sufficiently to accommodate another person in your daily life. If your LTA breaks up, you will have validated your own needs, and instead of regarding the breakup as a sign of "failure," you will have used your LTA creatively.

FROM RAINBOW EXPECTATIONS TO GRAY REALITIES

The living together arrangement itself guarantees nothing. The guarantee resides in what you and your partner make of it. You can guarantee it to be a creative experience *or* a shambles, depending on your expectations and your awareness of what is involved in an LTA *before* you enter into it. You can easily be trapped by unrealistic expectations, even though you enter such an arrangement voluntarily, if you simply "drift" into living together.

Dr. James Purcell, a colleague of mine, has worked with many LTAers and found that all too frequently, in his words, "a drifting process" took place.* Here are typical examples of the way some of these men and women explained how they started to live together:

□ "It didn't really seem to be a decision—it just evolved. We saw each other a few times, then we started living together, and he started staying at my place more and more."

□ "It was just easier. I wanted a pleasant dinner when I could get it. It was convenient."

□ "I maintained a separate apartment as a cover for parents. When our friends accepted it, I guess we were really living together."

□ "We never really decided. All of a sudden everything was there, that's all. I said to him: 'Give me some closet space.' That was decisive. Also when we bought a bureau. I think when a mutual friend got married I mentally moved in."

□ "She decided to move in. I was against it. I thought my privacy and independence would be taken away."

□ "We spent a year apart and I was very lonely in this community of people around the school where I was teaching. Everybody was married. I was ready to live with someone."

When people drift into a living-together arrangement, the LTA may become a staging area for new difficulties

---

*I am indebted to Dr. Purcell for making available to me his doctoral thesis (unpublished), titled: *Illusion and Reality: A Closer Look at the Dynamics of Cohabitation, Marriage and Commitment*, in which these examples of the drifting process were given.

rather than a mutual opportunity for self-enhancement. Couples think they can get "more" out of life by living together in a voluntary arrangement. But as Dr. Purcell discovered, "certainly these couples did get more—more sex, more contact, more love *and more pain*." Arguments, conflicts, and disagreements increase the longer they live together, while the sex, the contact, and the love diminish. Breaking up becomes a time of hurt, puzzlement, and confusion rather than a positive learning experience.

People who drift into a living-together arrangement usually think that since the arrangement is voluntary, they are protected against difficulties or rejection. They are free spirits; they can leave at any time, since no legalities are involved. The living-together arrangement will provide the happiness they want, and if not, well then, "so long—it's been good to know you." But both parties discover that love and intimacy demand a far higher price than they are prepared to pay.

In my LTLA Seminars many men and women indicate that they suffered from what I can only call "LTA shock." Instead of the living-together arrangement improving their relationship, as they had hoped and believed it would, their relationship deteriorated into a blame-making and bad feelings similar to what they had experienced in their previous marriages. For example:

Wendy started making demands. Jack felt "stir-happy" from around-the-clock togetherness. Corrinne reflects that her LTA partner, who was such a fun person before they lived together, showed himself to be irresponsible and incapable of making decisions. Eric thought his and his partner's sex life would improve since it wasn't that great before they lived together, but instead it got worse. Cindy sees herself as ripped off because her partner never listened to her concerns; he would sulk, walk away, and turn on the TV in the other room. Gary felt rejected and taken advantage of when his partner decided to quit work and return full time to school to get a college degree. Nancy acted just like her mother when she found herself attacking her partner for not having enough get-up-and-go spirit when he became unemployed. . . .

And then there were the unexpected little things that drove them up the wall: He is a night owl; she is an early-to-bedder. He likes well-done meat; she likes it rare. He likes classical music; she likes rock. He drops his clothes anywhere and splashes in the bathroom like a duck; she insists on a place for everything and demands a spotless bathroom. He is a meat and potatoes man; she is a vegetarian. He prefers to decorate a room in his favorite color, green; she is passionate about pink and can't abide green. He buys a lounge chair; she wanted a table instead. He squeezes the toothpaste wastefully from the top; she squeezes it economically from the bottom. He is silent in the morning and drinks only a cup of coffee for breakfast; she is chirpy from the moment she wakes up and loves huge breakfasts.

When romantic expectations vanish in the process of living together, these molehills turn into mountains of discontent. But the greatest LTA shock is still to come. This happens when the pair breaks up. I can still hear the pain and puzzlement in Ellen's voice when she told the members of her LTLA group:

"Gene and I broke up a month ago after living together for two years. I feel absolutely miserable about it even though I was the one who said I couldn't stand his jealousy and possessiveness any longer. I keep asking myself why should I feel so miserable? After all, Gene and I went into our relationship with no strings attached. We even said we were free spirits—we wanted it that way, because we didn't want to repeat what our past marriages were like. I had been quite open with all my friends about the fact that Gene and I were going to live together, even before we rented an apartment. They approved 100 percent. They said how great it was that we were going into the relationship without any commitments. Just staying with each other as long as it pleased us with none of the legal hassles of a divorce to get in the way. But it has not worked out that way. I feel I've lost something since we split. I invested more of myself in the relationship than I realized. Maybe I had been fooling myself, because I cry now that I'm alone. I really thought we would be together for a long, long time and now it's over. Would you believe it—when my friends heard about my leaving Gene, they congratulated me! They said that I was home free, a nice clean finish, because I didn't make any commitment to the relationship in the first place. I wanted sympathy from them, because I was really hurting, but they were saying I should be happy. Even my best friend, Jane, couldn't understand me when I told her that the breakup felt even worse than my divorce. It was as if all my hopes were smashed. I should be happy it ended because I went into the relationship with no strings attached. I don't know . . . maybe she's right.

Since the relationship ended, I've discovered breaking up is sticky legally, even though we were not married. That's because Gene has become very bitter. He's no longer the man I thought he was when we first met. He has refused to give me the stereo set and records and the expensive dinnerware I bought with my own money. Much as I hate to do it, I've decided to go to a lawyer to see if I can get my property back. I never wanted to see a lawyer again after my divorce, yet here I am becoming involved with them again!''

For Ellen, as well as for many others who drift into an LTA, this turbulence was entirely unexpected. She and Gene had never talked before living together about value differences (she wanted the freedom to date; Gene wanted a monogamous relationship), about money and buying arrangements, about recognizing and accommodating to each other's different life-styles (Gene was a night owl—she was an early-to-bedder). But most unexpected of all was the deep pain she felt. They had made no commitments to each other. The breakup "should" have been painless. They weren't married so there were no legal ties to dissolve. But Ellen found out that the lack of a marriage license doesn't guarantee a painless breakup. She had become emotionally involved in spite of the lightheartedness with which she had begun the LTA. Emotional involvement is not a spigot one can turn on and off at one's convenience.

One of the reasons Ellen's breakup was more painful than her divorce is the lack of support she is getting from her friends. They believe the relationship was trivial because it wasn't legal. At least society validated the fact that her marriage had been important, since legalities were involved. But an LTA has no definite status in the eyes of the law. Ellen felt guilty about wanting sympathetic recognition from her friends that her deepest feelings were involved. Of course, Ellen has "the right" to feel pain. She shared her life with another person for two years, and emotions and commitments change significantly in that period of time. Thus, the relationship and its breakup were important experiences in her life, not trivial episodes. When Ellen accepts this reality, she will no longer feel guilty about having the painful feelings she thinks she should not have. For just like a marriage that ends in a divorce, the breakup of a living-together arrangement must be mourned and laid to rest in one's feelings.

THE REAPPEARANCE OF LEGAL PROBLEMS

Ellen was shocked that once again she was becoming involved in a legal wrangle. In order to understand how LTAers can get involved in legal confrontations, I sought out Beverly Savitt, an outstanding Marin County, California, lawyer who has handled many LTA breakup cases. Her analysis and suggestions reported below afford food for thought to any man or woman involved in or considering a living-together arrangement:

"There is the illusion among many unmarried people when they decide to live together of 'If I don't get married, I don't have to get divorced. I don't have to go to court and the judge isn't going to tell me what I have to do. So we can live together, or we can decide to separate, without being bothered with what a judge says.' But when a breakup actually occurs, they may find themselves hiring two lawyers and facing one judge. The reality is that each of them, while they were living together, did something for each other that entailed services or money. One or both may become angry with each other when they split up. For example, the woman may have given up her own job and devoted full time to being a homemaker, while the man may have supplied all the money; or they may have made an oral agreement regarding future finances. But now they feel ripped off and look to their lawyers for 'justice.' I can recall a recent case in which one of the parties kept calling up and threatening his former partner with physical abuse or arrest. Why? Well he claimed that she had taken without his permission some joint property out of the house in which they had lived. It turned into a legal battle similar to a divorce case.

"Lawyers again enter into the picture when children are involved. Not infrequently the ex-wife will not allow the children an overnight visitation with their father because he is 'living in sin' with a woman friend. In one court case the mother objected to such overnight visitation when, in fact, the father had insufficient funds to live by himself—he had to have a roommate. But he was being punished for the fact that his roommate was a woman. Incidentally, the judge denied overnight visitation, which was totally unfair to the father and to his children.

"Because laws differ in each state I would recommend that both parties see a lawyer and become fully informed about the legal status of a living-together arrangement in their community before they start living together. I would also recommend that they draw up a pre-living-together-arrangement agreement to prevent possible future legal conflicts over money or property. In community-property states, people should understand what "separate property" and "community property" rights mean in case of a breakup. What happens if you mingle the two types of property is also essential for them to know. In other states, there should be concern for the law on common-law marriages for possible rights created through oral promises to each other. Of course I have heard people say this is not a romantic thing to do—contracts and love don't mix. But I think, in a way, it is *more* romantic because what you are saying by having such an agreement is: 'I am with you because I love you and not because of your money.' I think a person with a substantial amount of property may be asking himself or herself, 'Do you love me or just my money?' A pre-living-together-arrangement agreement can lay that concern to rest. Then they can get on with living together without the concern of what is going to happen to them economically if it breaks up. That concern is implicit in a living-together arrangement because people enter into such an arrangement in the first place with the idea that it may not be permanent. A pre-living-together-arrangement agreement can prevent some of that anxiety from interfering with the relationship.''

Ms. Savitt's comments indicate that where questions of love and intimacy are involved, nothing is as simple as it may seem. Regardless of whether or not you and your partner draw up a written contract, it is important to be aware of the possible legal implications of your arrangement.

As I shall subsequently show, the living-together arrangement can be used creatively as a bridge to a creative commitment. But before that can happen, the couple must be aware of its possible complexities and pitfalls if they are to enhance, rather than diminish, their lives.

MAKING AN LTA A CREATIVE LEARNING EXPERIENCE

Certainly a living-together arrangement is not for those who expect the arrangement itself to provide the stability and emotional satisfaction that can only be provided by the two people out of their own inner resources. This expectation is no different from the belief that a marriage ceremony insures happiness ever after. I am reminded of a statement made by the *eighth* wife of actor Mickey Rooney, who said she married him because "Mickey believes so much in the institution of marriage—I can't disappoint him." For many, the LTA has served as a modern version of Mickey Rooney's marriage expectations, much to their disillusionment. However, for many others, an LTA can be a creative learning experience. This is particularly true for those men and women who have been for some time in the selective-distancing third stage of learning to love again and have begun to feel the need for a more stable arrangement with one special person. Their feelings may be mixed: they may still find it difficult to trust themselves or another person to make a creative commitment; they may still be hesitant about modifying their single-person life-style to accommodate another person; they may still fear loss of freedom in another "togetherness" trap. But the push within themselves to take the risk of sharing room and board without pledging permanence exceeds the pull to remain in the selective-distancing stage.

If you believe you are ready to engage in an LTA, the complications and risks that may be involved need not deter you. Regardless of the type of relationship, the road to a creative commitment is to some degree chancy and frightening. The major positive advantage of an LTA is that it focuses both partners' attention on personal responsibility. You and your partner will live together out of choice, not because society forces you to. Either of you can leave the relationship when it is no longer satisfying. This realization will alert both of you to recognize that your relationship has to be renewed each day in order to establish something that is stable, trusting, and mutually satisfying. Under such circumstances, neither of you can take each other for granted. Therefore, both of you have to use the best of yourselves in order to make the relationship work: Your self-awareness, sensitivity, empathy, flexibility, openness, realism, and capacity to cope with the unexpected, plus a sense of humor derived from the knowledge that nobody is perfect. Should some of these qualities seem to be rusty, the LTA offers you an excellent opportunity to make them glisten again. Allowing them to remain rusty will serve only to rust the relationship.

For your living-together arrangement to become a stepping-stone toward the creation of a lasting love commitment, both of you should be clear in advance about why you are making this choice. For example, Pat and I did not ''drift'' into our arrangement. We had known each other for at least two years. Both of us were in the selective-distancing stage of learning to love again but felt ready to move a step beyond that stage. We wanted something more than our dating arrangement was affording us. We wanted to eliminate the inconvenience of dating that involved leaving each other three or four nights a week at 3 A.M. in order to get to our 8 A.M. jobs the next day and missing each other the rest of the time. We liked the idea that living together would enable us to satisfy our sexual needs when they would arise rather than at inconvenient dating times. We looked forward to being able to count on the stable presence and emotional support of the other in sharing our hopes and dreams and uncertainties. The possibility of each of us being available to the other for the renewal of our courage and the solution of our difficulties made living together sound like the natural next step in our relationship. But we had many fears and hesitations. Our hopes sounded lovely, but would the reality prove otherwise? We wouldn't know until we took the risk. We did know, however, that we were not prepared to get married. We did not trust ourselves or each other enough at that time to believe we were really capable of eliminating the lifelong learned habits of blaming or sulking whenever we were unhappy. Could we really practice open communication about stressful differences between us (differences we were bound to experience because they happen in any relationship) and risk being rejected and unloved? Neither of us could answer these fundamental questions in advance. They could only be answered in the daily living of our relationship. A positive answer would mean the relationship could turn into a creative commitment; a negative answer could mean an eventual parting of the ways. We were, however, fully prepared for either eventuality. Both of us saw the LTA as an experimental stage that would prepare us for any development in each of our lives. We agreed that the relationship would be monogamous, but we did not enter into it with the unrealistic assumption that it "must" result in marriage or that it "must" be a short-term affair. The relationship would have no time limit and would be open to *any* possibility— marriage or a friendship or a breakup, depending on what both of us might decide. We did not think in terms of success or failure. Whatever might happen, both of us would be better persons for having experienced it. Should it result in marriage, it would be a marriage based on new ways of relating and loving. Should it result in friendship or a breakup, it would mean we had learned more about ourselves as human beings, and our increased self-awareness would improve our subsequent intimate relationships with the opposite sex. In any case, the LTA would be a creative learning experience.

If you decide to enter into a living-together arrangement and you and your partner wish to make it a creative learning experience, here are the major learning areas the two of you can focus on to improve the quality of your lives:

Learning to Consolidate Your Secure Single-Person Identity

An LTA can strengthen rather than weaken the security you have found in yourself since your divorce. At the beginning of an LTA you will probably feel like Pat and I did: We each kept one eye cocked on the exit door, fearing the undermining of our hard-earned personal freedom. This high degree of commitment anxiety was a product of old ways of relating and I-have-been-here-before feelings. Instead of seeing ourselves for what we were at the present time in our lives, we felt as if we still were the immature kids we were at the time of our first marriages. When we recognized that this was happening inside ourselves, we began to view our relationship in a more realistic way. Today was not yesterday, since we were more mature individuals who had already experienced creative divorces. We began to relax in the knowledge that no person could ever steal or swallow up our freedom to be separate individuals. We could only do that to ourselves. Each of us had to take responsibility for acting toward each other in ways that did not diminish the other as a human being. To take responsibility did not mean believing we were responsible for each other's happiness. "Responsibility" meant the ability to respond to the other person in ways that built up our own and the other's self-esteem, which in turn could create the happiness we desired.

The LTA allows for testing this approach. Should you at first experience a high degree of commitment anxiety, as we did, take a good look at that anxiety, discuss it openly with your partner, find out what it is telling you about yourself, and then deal with the findings constructively. The two of you will probably discover pockets of vulnerability that make you fear being swallowed up by the other person. Pat says this indeed happened to her. In the early months of our LTA, her pocket of vulnerability was her lack of assertiveness, which put stress on her and on our relationship.

"I was getting into the same old trap I was in when I was married," Pat says. "I was doing everything I thought Mel wanted me to do, even when I would rather do something else. I just went along and agreed with him, but I was becoming very resentful. However something very different from my previous marriage happened. When Mel began to feel my resentment, instead of keeping silent, he asked me if I wanted to talk about what was bothering me. Mel didn't automatically feel it was an attack against him. It was such a surprise and a relief for me to know that. So I told him that I was angry about his making commitments all the time for both of us to go to parties and meetings with people when I often didn't want to go. I'd rather sit home, read a book, or play my guitar. But I would always say yes even though I didn't mean it. I had been brought up with the belief that in order to keep the love of your man, you always do what he wants to do. Since my divorce I had established myself in many ways as an independent person. But I was finding out that when it came to being assertive, I was still the little girl who always had to conform and do what others wanted her to do if she were to retain their love.

"I learned, in sharing these feelings with Mel, that I

wasn't really angry with him, but with myself for feeling trapped into doing things with him that I didn't want to do. When Mel pointed out that he never knew I felt that way and that he had always asked me if I wanted to go to these affairs before he would make a commitment, I had to acknowledge that was true. I had no right to assume in advance he would be angry with me if I told him I didn't want to go, but that's what I'd been doing without even being aware of it. That's the advantage of talking heavy things out—you learn so much more about yourself when you have a receptive partner who really cares about you and doesn't feel threatened by disagreements.

"That talk with Mel made me take personal responsibility to change my way of behaving. At that time I was working at the Behavior Institute in Sausalito as the executive secretary and they were giving assertiveness training courses for men and women (it surprised me that many men were also unassertive). I began to look closely at some of the data I was typing concerning these courses and discovered that assertiveness was something you could *learn*. As a result of my talk with Mel, I decided to take the assertiveness training course. I must confess, I felt a little guilty when I told Mel this because I was still confusing assertiveness with becoming a pushy and aggressive person. But Mel said great, go ahead. He was supporting my desire to become independent and it wasn't a threat to him. That really was something new in my life. Well that course was one of the best things that ever happened to me. And it also improved our LTA relationship enormously. I discovered that there is all the difference in the world between being an assertive person and an aggressive one. Before I took the course I thought if I were assertive it might mean I would have to be selfish and hurt other people's feelings. On the contrary, being assertive means sticking up for my own rights and nipping things in the bud when I feel forced to do things I truly don't want to do. It involved taking greater charge over my own life rather than hurting other people's feelings.

"I didn't try out what I learned on Mel immediately, because when you learn new things it is kind of scary and you have to get used to them. I didn't want to fall flat on my face by acting hostile and aggressive toward him, but I did want to assert my needs. So I tried my assertiveness at first on small things that had always bothered me in my life—like the time at Macy's when I was standing in line in the accessories department. I was the next person in line to be waited on when all of a sudden a woman pushed her way in front of me and told the saleslady to take care of her glove purchase. Using what I learned from my assertiveness course, I tapped that woman on the shoulder and pleasantly said: 'I'm sorry but I believe I was next.' She turned around kind of surprised and apologized and then stepped back. To affirm my right to do this, I then said to the saleslady that I had been next in line.

"Now that sounds like such a simple, tiny thing, but for a woman like me who had always believed that asserting my rights was a pushy, hostile thing to do, it was a tremendous step forward. It was terribly difficult doing that the first time, since I felt I was performing a sinful act; I perspired, my heart stopped a beat, my stomach did flip-flops, my voice sounded shaky. But when it was over I felt pleased, because I did what was right and necessary for me, without attacking her by accusing her of being a gross, insensitive person. In the past my reaction to someone who cut in front of me would be to say nothing and allow her to remain. But oh how I used to boil over inside and fume over the nerve and audacity of some people. The more I would keep it inside myself the angrier I would get and it would spoil the rest of my day. What a waste of my energy!

"I also practiced my assertiveness with my friends. The first time I tried it out was when Michelle called up and asked me to come to another one of her Tupperware parties. Well I've been to what seems like a million Tupperware parties in my lifetime and just the thought of going to another one made me feel ill. I always used to go to them out of loyalty to my friends, but I used to feel resentful inside because they were imposing on me. This time I told Michelle, with a lump in my throat, that I had had my fill of Tupperware parties and wasn't interested in attending them any more, no matter who asked me. I could hardly believe I was saying that, because as soon as she asked me to attend I was thinking, 'Here I go again; she's making me feel guilty by saying she needs me, so I have to say I'll attend.' Instead, I handled the problem assertively by not attacking her but by putting the responsibility on myself.

"I could have zapped her with, 'Why do you always make me feel guilty because you want my attendance at your parties? I'm mad at you for even asking me to come to another one.' But when I simply said instead, without any lengthy explanations, that I'm sorry I can't attend, it felt as if an enormous burden were lifted from my shoulders. What surprised me most was that Michelle didn't sound put out at all. She accepted what I said with good grace. Nothing terrible happened and we're still the best of friends. If you have to hold a friendship at the expense of your own personhood, it really isn't worth keeping in the first place. That's even truer when you love someone.

"I had an opportunity shortly after my phone talk with Michelle to try out my new assertiveness with Mel. During the time of our LTA, Mel was a 'movie-holic.' He loved going out almost every night to catch the latest film. Whenever he had suggested that we see something, I always had agreed. Frequently, I didn't like the films he liked, because our tastes differ, but I never mentioned that to him. Nor did I mention the more important fact that my job demanded my sitting in a hard chair eight hours a day, so that the notion of sitting in a movie house for another three hours was something I didn't look forward to. Every time we went to a movie my backside would rebel, so I really wasn't very good company. Instead of making for a pleasant evening, moviegoing made me irritable, tired, and resentful. But I never had told Mel this because I thought if he really loves me he'll know what I've been feeling. However, all that changed one night when Mel made his usual suggestion of 'let's run out to the movies.' Instead of saying 'fine' like I used to, I shared my feelings with him. Before I did, however, I was worried. 'Maybe he'll think I don't love him if I don't do what he wants to do? Maybe he's a phony when he says he wants me to be assertive but will resent it when I show that I am?' These were the thoughts running through my mind. But I had gone too far in my new direction to stop now. My fears proved to be groundless. Instead, expressing my own feelings and needs cleared the air between us. I didn't attack him by saying, 'You're a selfish bastard for forcing me to go out with you when I don't want to.' That's the kind of nonsense that breaks up as many LTA's as keeping your feelings inside and becoming angry because you think your partner is forcing you to hide them. I told him instead, 'Dear, I just don't feel like sitting again for three hours' and explained my reasons. We were able to reach a compromise agreeable to both of us. Any time in the future if I didn't want to go I would say so and Mel was free to go alone or with a friend. He would enjoy himself and I would enjoy myself, since I had plenty of activities at home or with other friends that interested me. What I learned from this is that if two people in an LTA don't separate out their wants and needs, fights are bound to happen. You have to tell the other person where you are at, because that person wouldn't understand where you are at in a million years or how you are feeling if you keep silent. The surest way to break up a relationship is to believe the old notion that if a person loves you, he really would know what you are thinking. Nobody is a mind reader. I dropped that along with my nonassertiveness. Our LTA enabled me to do so. For myself, I've learned that Mel and I really are two different people who don't have to agree on everything and that our love can flourish on our differences as well as on our similarities. I've become more secure and independent by realizing this fact in the way we relate to each other. What is so exciting and hopeful is that I found out it doesn't make any difference how old you are. Here I was learning new ways and gaining new knowledge in my forties! Why, I used to think forty meant being over the hill. But now I know that anybody can change and grow at any time in life!

Learning to Cultivate Mindfulness

Mindfulness means widening your awareness of your own and your partner's needs, feelings, and boundaries. It also means sharing feelings, even though some of them may be negative, in a loving rather than hurtful way. The LTA can stimulate you to move in this direction because it is a voluntary arrangement that will break up if you simply repeat your past ways of relating to a loved person instead of improving in those ways. Of course, you are free to break it up quickly when difficulties arise, but then you will have to face the reality that each new relationship may end the same way. If you always assume the breakup is the other person's "fault," then each new relationship is like a piece of disposable tissue instead of an experience you can learn from. It is by dealing with the stress and strains of a relationship, rather than running away from them, that the groundwork for a truly creative commitment is established.

Many men and women continue to play the manipulative games that will eventually lead to a breakup. For example, there was Kevin, who told me: "I lived with Kate for two years. She seemed to be everything I needed. I am what you would call a passionate sportsman. I love skiing, boating, and tennis. As a matter of fact, I met Kate on a tennis court. She appeared to love all the sports I did, so when she said she would marry me, I thought, 'boy, am I lucky.' Now, dammit, I wish she had said no! We've been married six months and I've filed for divorce. Everything changed after our marriage. All of a sudden she became a homebody and said she didn't care much for sports but went along with me because I liked them. Not only that, instead of being the fun-loving woman I thought she was, she turned out to be deadly serious and began to criticize me all the time for being a spendthrift on my sports. She's just like my first wife— criticizing and complaining and trying to change me. It's like I never knew her in all the time we lived together before we married."

Kevin, of course, also had been playing a game since he had refused to see what was before his very eyes. Many clues in Kate's behavior before they were married indicated she was presenting a façade: Forced, strained smiles when she said how happy she was to be going on a ski trip; remarks about how nice it would be to save money and buy a house; her frequent illness the day before a boat race or ski trip; brief condemnatory looks when any of his friends' opinions about politics and morals displeased her.

Unless Kevin begins to cultivate the "mindfulness" needed to pick up nonverbal clues, he will feel deceived in every new relationship he enters into. He is already telling his friends that no woman can ever be trusted.

In addition to becoming mindful about the other person, it is necessary to share your negative feelings in a mindful way. Accusations and attacks only stimulate countercharges. No one likes to be humiliated. *How* you share your feelings and observations is even more important than what the feelings and observations are about. As Pat pointed out, she shared her negative feelings with me in an attempt to understand what was happening between us, so that we could remedy the difficulty. She did not attack me or accuse me of doing wrong. If she had, I might have attacked her in return. The problem we had to deal with and resolve would have been lost in the heat of our mutual recriminations.

Mindfulness also involves timing. The fact that two people live together doesn't mean that their needs are the same at the same time. Toleration and acceptance of differences in timing is essential, otherwise differences in timing will be translated into feelings of rejection. The fact that I am a night owl and Pat is an early-to-bedder doesn't mean that we reject each other. The fact that she may want to tell me immediately about something that bothers her, while I am still thinking about what happened at the office doesn't mean we are selfish and don't love each other. But we have to bring the difference out in the open, otherwise we will become resentment collectors. I have gotten into the habit of saying, "Honey, I know you have something important you want to tell me, and I want to hear it. But I've had a terribly tough day at the office and need to relax a while. Will it be okay to talk about it later when I can really give you my full attention?"

Pat does the same thing when I come on too strong at times. You may find it will work as well for you as it has for us. But don't say those words snappishly, harshly, or irritably. For even reasonable words can sound like an accusation if they are said with an overtone of resentment and hostility. When you realize your partner is simply in a different place from you in his or her feelings at that moment and is not rejecting you, you will be able to deal with the situation and your words will come out in a caring rather than an accusing fashion.

Mindfulness doesn't happen overnight. It is an activity that must be cultivated in a spirit of mutual goodwill and with the recognition that change will be gradual rather than instant. Mindfulness is learning a new habit which eventually becomes a natural part of your personality the longer you practice it. The effort is well worth making if both of you desire to move in the direction of a creative commitment. A mutual increase in mindfulness reinforces the sense of having secure single-person identities. The two of you can learn through the cultivation of mindfulness that there is nothing to fear but fear itself in the idea of a long-range sharing of two lives in an atmosphere of compassionate interdependency.

At that point a creative commitment can become a realistic possibility.

An LTA is a short-range life-style arrangement by its very nature. It is a testing ground that you can use to determine what kind of relationships fit best for you at this time in your life, though not necessarily for a later time. An LTA can enable you and your partner, through each other's feedback, to recognize and modify self-defeating behaviors in order to move toward a creative commitment, provided the desire to do so is present. Or it can serve as an interlude in which the desire to remain uncommitted or selectively distancing is reaffirmed. In either case, the LTA is no permanent solution, since it will lead to either a breakup or remarriage. There are some people who drift from a short-term LTA relationship into a long-term LTA who may vocally proclaim that this is not the case. Indeed, I have known a number of people who are currently in the seventh or eighth year of their LTA. These are monogamous couples who think, feel, and act like they are married. The lack of a piece of legal paper cannot conceal the reality of their relationship. A long-term LTA is no longer a living arrangement, but is really a marriage under another name.

For Pat and myself, the LTA enabled us, as it has enabled many others, to move in the direction of a creative commitment which involved remarriage. After living together for almost a year, we set our wedding date three months ahead. There are, however, many surprises in store for the not-so-recently divorced who decide to remarry. Pat and I were to experience these surprises, too, the closer our wedding date approached, as the next chapter will show.

6 Moving Toward a Creative Commitment

"Mel, I think you are a traitor!" These are the words I hear from a number of recently divorced men and women when I tell them I remarried almost four years after my divorce. As one woman put it to me:

"You have been telling people that a divorce, no matter how painful it might be, can be a creative experience. You also talk about the need for a divorced person like myself— I've been divorced one year—to become a whole person in my own right instead of a half person in a bad marriage. But now you've become a married person again. I don't think that is right. For me, the most important thing in life is to be a separate person, period."

I understand and sympathize with that woman. Two years after my own divorce I was accurately quoted in my local newspaper as saying I would never marry again. I invited Joan Lisetor, the writer of that news story, to my wedding party less than two years later. As a wedding gift, Joan gave me a framed copy of the news story in which I had said, "Never Again!"

Pat, too, experienced the same "marriage-ugh" attitude. But by the time we married, we had arrived at a point in our lives where we were both grateful for Joan's gift, as Joan well knew we would be. That framed article now hangs in our bedroom as a constant reminder to both of us to "never say never." Strong feelings and strong convictions are not forever. It was "right" for Pat and me to feel negatively about marriage when we were living through the process of proving that we could survive emotionally and physically by ourselves. And it is "right" for the woman who challenged me to feel that continuing to establish her separate identity is the most important thing in her life right now. But when she becomes comfortable with her hard-earned sense of personal identity, it may not be "right." It may then be "right" for her to consider whether or not a living-together arrangement or remarriage poses a threat or a promise to her sense of who she is.

It had taken me much time to realize that becoming comfortable with myself as a separate person did not mean the end of the idea of committing myself to loving another person. There is no contradiction between these two ideas, since a whole-person identity is the necessary foundation for a lasting, meaningful relationship. What is "right" at one stage in our life may very well prove "wrong" and self-defeating at the *next* stage. Pat's and my decision to remarry required us to reassess our outlook on marriage rather than to act without thinking on the old "marriage-ugh" attitude.

FROM THE FRYING PAN INTO THE FIRE?

Marriage the second time around can be different from the first in many unexpected ways, as Pat and I were to find out. We had been living together for almost a year when Pat proposed to me. Here is how Pat saw it:

"Just like life is a process of growing and going on to other things, I felt that we had grown so close that I, for one, was ready to take the next step. I felt the need for a ceremony to rejoice before the world over the fact that we had lived together for almost a year and that we liked and loved each other even more as a result. To be married would be like the frosting on the cake.

"I wasn't trying to put a gun to your head when I said, 'I would like you to marry me, Mel.' It wasn't as if I were giving you an ultimatum such as 'Why haven't you asked me to marry you? You know you have a pretty neat person here, so stop playing games.' I wasn't telling you how you should feel; I was telling you what I was feeling. I wasn't trying to manipulate you. I had spent too many years of my adult life manipulating others, like so many other women have been forced by society to do. I used to cry or play the clown or perform my cute-dumb-helpless little girl bit in order to get my way. I hated myself for doing that. It's a childish thing to do because when you manipulate others all you get is a dislike for yourself.

"Instead, I was just naturally expressing to you what I deeply felt. If I hadn't taken that assertiveness training course while we were living together, I would have been too scared to say what I was feeling about you. You and I came from a generation that considers marriage the deepest commitment and I felt that you too were toying with the idea. As a matter of fact, you would say from time to time: 'Living like this is almost like being married to you.' And you were saying that, not with a sour expression on your face, but rather like marriage might not be too bad an idea after all. But I felt that even if you rejected my idea of wanting to get married, that wouldn't mean the end of the world for me. If you didn't want that kind of a commitment, and I did, that meant that we were two different people who felt differently about what was happening between us. It would not mean you were a 'meanie,' while I was 'the nice person.' We would openly talk out our differences, just as we have done with so many other issues in our life together, and see where we would go from there.''

I wasn't really surprised to hear Pat voice her desire to get married, because I had been thinking the same thought for a month before the issue came out into the open. But I was trying to first feel comfortable inside myself with the idea of marrying again. That was no easy task. Feelings of failure and guilt about a "failed" marriage began to pop into my mind again, after I thought they had long since disappeared. It was Ambrose Bierce's definition of marriage that kept tap-dancing around in my head: "The state or condition of a community consisting of a master, a mistress, and two slaves, making in all, two.''

However, the realities of our present living-together arrangement indicated that a marriage commitment could perhaps be practiced in new ways. We had decided to enter into our living-together arrangement without any strings attached, other than that it was to be monogamous while it lasted; we had imposed no time limit on the arrangement; and we did not live together in order to prepare for marriage. We were taking one day at a time and were enriching each other's lives by being as open, sensitive, and respectful of each other's needs as we could be. We had often talked about our belief that a lasting, enlivening relationship could only happen if the relationship was renewed each day by our caring, empathic concern for each other. We put our talk into action and it worked. We jealously guarded our newfound sense of being whole persons and were excessively sensitive to the slightest sign that either was being used as an extension of the other's needs. But instead of sweeping such slights, imagined or otherwise, under the rug until the dust would have choked us, we voiced our feelings openly as soon as they occurred and found we could resolve disagreements constructively. And we had no desire to tomcat around; monogamous sex fulfilled our needs in a way promiscuity could never do. Our sex life was the confirmation of a deepening commitment to each other, which made sex so much more gratifying than the mere release of physical tension. In effect, we were experiencing a *creative* commitment to each other. It was "creative" in the sense that we were creating new ways of relating to each other that enhanced rather than diminished our relationship.

Then why get married? What is so important about a piece of paper? One reason I got married was that I began to realize that the institution itself does not cause the agony. It is the way two people relate to each other within the marriage framework that causes the difficulties. To think otherwise is like blaming the building a restaurant is in for an atrocious dinner prepared by an incompetent chef. Marriage fills the need of a person like myself for a reinforcing sense of community and structure. Marriage can be a celebration: an acknowledgment to oneself and to society that one is making one of the deepest commitments one can ever make. What could be more important than the commitment to share the widest range of who one is with another person? That kind of commitment, of course, is not for everyone. But for people like myself and Pat, and for millions of others, it is infinitely valuable and desirable.

I thought it might prove possible, after all, to use marriage constructively as reinforcement of a creative commitment rather than as a jailhouse for two. For what was new in Pat's and my approach to our marriage was that we were *not* marrying in order to become "acceptable" in the eyes of other people. We were *not* marrying because society said "it is time" for the two of you to marry, presenting us with a tax advantage as a wedding gift from the government. We were *not* marrying because the world around us looks like a Noah's Ark of twosomes, particularly around Thanksgiving and Christmas. Neither were we marrying because we had fallen in love with the idea of instant romantic love. After all, it had taken us almost four years of growing into loving each other to reach this new stage in our relationship. Nor were we viewing marriage as a "solution" to all of our problems. Instead, we were making a marital commitment because it was a validation of our shared experience. We learned from our living-together arrangement that we could grow separately and together as human beings. Now, we wanted to deepen our commitment. We chose to marry because each of us felt like whole persons, rather than like half-persons a marriage would make whole.

A living-together arrangement, even at its best, doesn't

allow for the deepest kind of creative commitment two people can experience. In the back of the mind there is always a little voice saying: "I can always split from this relationship when the going gets rough. There is no need to make year-from-now plans about what we will do together, since we may not be together tomorrow." The difficult issues can be avoided or evaded. To be creatively committed to each other is to recognize that there is a darker side of love, where two people grow as human beings in the process of working out wrenching conflicts of interest and very painful disagreements. Resolving these difficulties binds the partners closer: the love becomes richer; the sharing and caring increases in sensitivity and appropriateness. The LTA relationships rarely move into and through extreme difficulties toward a brighter horizon. They usually terminate at the point where they could have become deeper. As this chapter will show, Pat and I experienced this basic difference between marriage and an LTA more than once after we married each other.

Now that Pat and I had faced the challenge of marriage and decided to accept it, could we deepen our love and make it last within a framework that hadn't proved too workable before? All we could do would be to try.

REMARRIAGE SHOCK

When Pat and I were divorced from our first spouses, we experienced "separation shock," as I termed it in *Creative Divorce*. Separation shock is the unexpected fear and vulnerability newly divorced men and women feel when they realize they now have to survive on their own but don't quite believe they can.

Pat and I now discovered that there is such a thing as "getting-together shock" that is almost as upsetting, if not as long lasting, as a separation shock. "Remarriage shock" is my name for it, and in some ways it is more surprising than separation shock because it is even more unexpected.

The ceremony was to occur at 2 P.M. on Sunday, October 21, 1973. I felt sure that I was taking the right step, even though I had to step lightly on my bandaged right foot. Pat exuded radiance and serenity. Everything seemed in order. We were marrying on the lawn of a house in Berkeley, California, owned by friends of ours, Jim and Helen Maas. They had generously offered us its use and had agreed to serve as our witnesses. The ceremony was to be private—just the four of us and the priest who had also married them. We planned to hold a large wedding celebration with our friends and relatives two weeks later. Jim and Helen had married for the second time a year before we did. Like Pat and me, they are in their middle years and had lived together before their marriage.

Pat and I had intently watched the pushes and pulls of Jim and Helen's relationship. When they married, we asked ourselves: Would their marriage destroy the friendship and love they had established in their living-together relationship? Would the legal piece of paper they had signed be a noose around their necks?

The similarities of their developing relationship to our own accounted for our more than passing interest in their remarriage experience. Seeing that the quality of their lives together had improved during the first year of their remarriage powerfully reinforced our own decision to re-marry.

At 2:00 we stood on a lawn resplendent in sunshiny October California weather. We looked into the pleasant face of the informally dressed priest, who was marrying us in the words we chose for the ceremony. These words emphasized that we were committing ourselves to the sharing of the widest range of who we were as human beings. That we were whole persons coming together to grow as independent human beings in a bond of mutual interdependency. It was a nontraditional ceremony (I am Jewish and Pat is Catholic). But we wanted the ceremony to stress that the spirit as well as the flesh was involved in our relationship, hence the presence of a warm and understanding priest.

The ceremony took less than ten minutes—but it felt like ten years. That was our first surprise. The second surprise was that halfway through the ceremony my insides turned into a puddle of fear, which Pat later told me also happened to her. It was as if I were losing my balance, the ground beneath me shaking like an earthquake. Oh-my-God-what-am-I-doing-here? feelings rushed through me. My vision blurred. Pat was little help when I struggled to place the wedding ring on her left hand; her left hand was bobbing around like a canoe in turbulent waters. I finally fit the ring on her finger, but I hardly felt proud of my performance. What kind of a whole person was I who could turn to Jell-O so suddenly?

We had expected to be exhilarated, but only the witness-es seemed to have festive feelings. They had prepared an elegant early dinner for us, with champagne toasts for open-ers. Pat and I quickly put on our best smiling faces as we listened to the warmhearted toasts, drank the fine champagne, and ate the gourmet food. But our faces were masks hiding the inexplicable emotional uproar inside ourselves. Shortly after dinner, Pat became very pale. She got up, said "Please excuse me, I need some fresh air. In fact I need more than fresh air," and made a wobbly exit. I quickly followed her outside the back door and asked her what was the matter. She gasped: "Could you get me a container? I'm going to throw up right now!"

I yelled for a bucket and Jim came to the rescue, placing a plastic Kelly-green bucket in front of Pat. When we returned inside some minutes later, Pat apologized. "I'm so very sorry, please forgive me. I felt very nauseous and threw up in the bucket." Jim replied with compassionate humor, "That's all right, Pat. You know, you are the neatest thrower-upper we have ever had over here. It all went into the bucket, you didn't spill a drop!"

Pat wanted to lie down. I helped her walk to the bedroom and suddenly realized how terribly tired and dizzy *I* was. We lay down, side by side, still dressed in our wedding-day finery, with exhaustion rather than romance on our minds. We slept from 5 P.M. to midnight. Our understanding friends, who knew our actions were not a comment on their superb hospitality, closed the bedroom door and let us sleep.

When we got up, we made our embarrassed apologies to our hosts and drove to the lodge where we had honeymoon reservations. When we woke the next day, it was as if we were suddenly strangers. We were awkward, clumsy, and tense. It took Pat and me the rest of that first week before we started to become what we had been to each other (and to ourselves) before the marriage ceremony.

THE WHY OF WHAT HAPPENED

Pat and I had experienced a temporary identity jolt: "Who were we now that we were married again?"

We worried about our identities. For us, as for many others, the social roles people take on, or leave, or lose at various times in their lives define for them, to a considerable degree, how they see themselves. A divorced woman may feel she has no identity when she no longer has the role of wife, and she may call herself worthless. But as she takes on the new role of a single person and proves her ability to survive on her own, she may see herself as an independent human being, valuable in her own right.

Pat and I had lost our married-person roles when we were divorced. Now we thought we were losing the single-person roles we had so painfully built for ourselves for almost four years. We had associated marriage with failure. Was all the hard work we undertook to make ourselves whole now to be wasted effort? It seemed so to us those first days of our remarriage. All our brave words and actions seemed forgotten in the scary reality of our new togetherness.

We had not realized a marriage ceremony could be so upsetting for divorced people. It took us some time to sort out the reasons why this would inevitably be true, not only for ourselves, but for many men and women who remarry. For marriage still remains the ultimate commitment two people make to each other. In a marriage we put our whole sense of who we are on the line for observation and acceptance by our spouse. Will he or she value me, respect me, understand me, like me, comfort me, reassure me, reinforce me, protect me—in the special loving way that can only be realized through marriage?

These questions are very different for second-time-around people than for first-time-arounders. We experienced marriage before and felt damaged when it ended. We frequently attached the label "loser" to ourselves and to other divorced people in the first two years after the marriage ended. And now, it felt to Pat and me as if we were reliving the past. We seemed to have become fragile, helpless victims riding a roller coaster to another divorce. We felt we had "given up" our single-person identities with the marriage ceremony. All we had left, it seemed, was a feeling we could no longer relate positively to each other now that we were married.

In my counseling work with men and women who are considering remarriage, I have found that "remarriage shock" frequently causes the relationship to end before the remarriage date. Linda, an attractive, thirty-one-year-old nurse, had been divorced five years. She and Don, whom she had been going with for one year, set the wedding date four months in advance. As the date drew closer, she felt increasingly uneasy about the relationship. She was puzzled, since she had been more active in the affair and had felt gratified that she had overcome *his* resistance to remarriage. "But after he agreed, I didn't feel as happy as I thought I should have felt," she said. "In fact, now that I got what I wanted, I felt I really didn't want it that much after all, if you know what I mean. Then I suddenly wanted to go out and sleep with other men. That was kind of odd of me because Don is a real good lover and we had a monogamous relationship, which I liked all the time I had been going with him. Well, I did start playing around without telling Don, after we had set the marriage date. And wouldn't you know it, Don caught sight of me and Harry (that's who I started to sleep with) going into a motel one day. And that ended our relationship. The sex was okay with Harry, but was much better with Don. I don't know why I did it. I loved Don, maybe I still do, but I'm sure making a mess of things.''

What happened to Linda before remarriage was very similar to what happened to Pat and me after our marriage. There was the same feeling of anxiety about giving up personal identity. In Linda, the anxiety proved overwhelming and destroyed a relationship that the healthy part of her wanted so very much to continue.

While Linda's reaction to the prospect of her new marriage was excessive, her feelings of anxiety and her desire to flee the situation are typical and normal, given the significance of the new commitment. If we can learn to recognize these feelings for what they are, they can be used to improve the marital commitment, rather than destroy it. Though these feelings seem to tell you that you will lose your personhood and repeat the self-defeating behavior that wrecked your previous marriage, they are really saying: ''Hey, wait a minute! This jolt I'm giving you is to wake you up and force you to reexamine who you are today, *not* what you were yesterday. Take a *new* look at what your marriage will be all about. You have the potential to make it a life-enhancing or hellish experience. You can't put the responsibility for how you relate to your loved one on anyone but yourself.''

Remarriage shock is not infrequently expressed a few months *after* a remarriage. As Janice put it: ''Once I had made the decision to remarry I felt calm and content and the honeymoon days were very good. But then we started to grate on each other's nerves and I began to see what a huge gap in knowledge I had about my new husband. When he started to put me down all the time and give me written schedules I had to follow like a little schoolgirl, it really hit me that I was losing my individuality that I had built up in the four years after my divorce. That was two months after we married and I felt I had given up the most valuable thing I had, which was myself. It really frightened me, losing who I was. I had had that happen in my first marriage. I took fourteen years of that kind of garbage from my first husband and I wasn't going to allow that to happen again. We're separated now. Maybe there's a chance for us yet if he really understands that I'm a person too and that I have to be treated like an equal. I thought he wanted that kind of a relationship when we were dating. Well, it's best that I know now rather than fourteen years from now whether that was my fantasy trip or whether we can change the way we are chewing each other up.''

When properly understood, remarriage shock can enhance a relationship rather than destroy it. Remarriage shock means something far more positive than first appears. When Janice told her story, she was telling herself that she was *not* the same person she had been in her marriage. She is a separate person worthy of being treated with respect. In recognizing her remarriage shock, Janice honestly confronted a basic issue of marriage that needs to be resolved in the early months, rather than be suffered through for the rest of one's life.

MISLEARNING FROM THE PAST

There is a prevalent virus I call "mislearning from the past," to which the not-so-recently divorced are very susceptible. This virus had caused me to repeatedly say I could never marry again. I had forgotten Mark Twain's insight: "We should be careful to get out of an experience only the wisdom that is in it—and stay there, lest we be like the cat that sits down on a hot stove-lid. She will never sit down on a hot stove-lid again, and that's well—but also, she will never sit down on a cold one any more!"

To assume that a new marriage will simply repeat the past is to mislearn from the past. Remarriage shock can jolt you into examining how your new marriage can offer you the opportunity to improve on the past.

The jolt of our remarriage forced Pat and me to face up to, and honestly answer, the following questions that are central to determining the survival potential of any remarriage:

□ *Are you the same person today that you were in your previous marriage?*

Of course not, but you may think you are when you decide to enter a relationship that has the same name ("marriage") and the same legalities attached to it as your previous marriage. If you do not realize you have changed, your remarriage could very well repeat your previous marriage. Dramatist Max Frisch has observed that when you think you know your future because of your past experience, then "your behavior is not governed by the present, but by a memory. . . . That's why it turned out to be the same story every time."

But you have established a whole-person identity for

yourself since your previous marriage; *that* is the reality of who you are today. The feeling that you are a helpless, vulnerable person, liable to fail in the new relationship, is an echo from your past. To identify and acknowledge it as the past masquerading as the present eliminates its power to destroy your new relationship. You bring to your new marriage the strength of having survived on your own since your divorce. Consequently, you do not bring the false expectation that your spouse must and will satisfy every conceivable need in your life, an expectation on which so many marriages founder.

◻   *What have you learned from your previous marriage?*

If you have learned only negatives from your past marriage, your new marriage will be in deep trouble. As one woman said to me: "Unless I have already filled up my own cup, what can I share with another person? In my past marriage, I felt at the time it ended like a deprived person. It was as if my husband had deprived me of my trust in myself and of my love for him. Now that I've been divorced four years, I see my first marriage in a more positive light. It's not that I don't see the bad parts of that marriage for what they were; they were bad, period. But I also see now that my husband and I were well-intentioned people. We didn't mean to create a hell for each other. In fact, we loved each other to the best of our ability, but we were really ignorant about how to go about maintaining a good relationship. And I also know that I learned in my marriage to give and receive love. We loved to the best of our ability then, but our ability was limited by our lack of knowledge and our illusions. Planning and sharing my life with another person can be a turn-on that living alone doesn't give me. I learned that too in my marriage. That my marriage ended isn't as important to me now as knowing that maybe I can apply the good things I experienced in it to my new relationship and eliminate the bad things. I think I'm wiser now.''

WHAT ABOUT OPEN MARRIAGE?

Open marriage has come to mean that extramarital affairs are an acceptable way to make your marriage work. Since all men and women experience lust in their hearts at times (as a famous politician acknowledges), extramarital relationships may seem like a good idea. In practice, however, they are a time bomb that explodes the marriage they are intended to improve. Sex is an expression of intimacy and trust in a committed relationship. Promiscuity wipes out the trust that exists. Before marrying Pat, I knew from my experience as a counselor that divorce was usually the consequence of an open marriage, even when the husband and wife agreed to each other's affairs.

Like many couples who try to ''save'' their unsatisfactory marriages by having another child, open-marriage couples try to ''save'' their relationships by having other sexual partners. But instead of enhancing their relationships, these actions diminish the possibility of maintaining their marriages.

ARE YOU BRINGING HIDDEN AGENDAS TO YOUR REMARRIAGE?

Hidden agendas are the private expectations you may have about how your new marriage "should" work. You have not discussed them with your new spouse before remarriage because you sensed they might produce disagreement and conflict. Because you hope to live happily ever after, you convince yourself that these problems will solve themselves. Usually hidden agendas are a list of "give-me's" that might cause your partner to say, "Hey, you're asking for everything from me, but you're not considering my point of view." Hidden agendas range from "I expect you to remain monogamous while I can have as many extramarital affairs as I want" to "I'm going to be in control of all the money since I'm the wage earner" to "I expect you to keep a super-clean house and have dinner on the table at six o'clock on the dot" to "I want to have a child but I'd better hold off mentioning it until after we are married."

Holding on to a hidden agenda is a sure road to a quick divorce after a remarriage. Nothing undermines the trust of the other party in the relationship more than the hiding of issues that should be discussed.

HOW MUCH DO YOU REALLY KNOW ABOUT THE PERSON YOU ARE MARRYING?

If you answer, "Why everything worth knowing of course," stop a minute. Didn't you assume you knew your spouse in your previous marriage like an open book—and then found out that the book was written in a foreign language? Too many divorced people, like myself, did exactly that.

Echoing through my mind are the dazed comments of the hundreds of recently divorced people in my Creative Divorce Seminars who say, "I always thought we had such a good marriage, but he just told me that in most of the years of the marriage he was absolutely miserable. I don't think I ever really knew the man. He seems like such a stranger to me now."

If there has been one piece of knowledge burned into my soul from my own first marriage, it is this: Never think you know in advance what your spouse is thinking or feeling or the reasons why your spouse is acting in a certain way. You have no right to believe you are a mind reader any more than your spouse has that right. As a nightclub act, mind reading has its merits, but as a basis for relating effectively in a marriage it has none whatsoever. A remarriage, to be lasting and fulfilling, must acknowledge that fact as a bedrock of the relationship.

Pat and I didn't know "everything" about each other when we married. And there are parts of us that perhaps we will never reveal, since they are private to ourselves and do not affect our relationship. But we thought we knew enough about each other to give marriage another try. We did not see each other as fixed-for-all-time personalities. Instead we saw each other as two separate individuals in the process of change and growth who felt we could grow more richly together than alone. We liked what we saw in each other, but we also recognized we had shown each other little more than a small part of ourselves. For each of us, remarriage would be a voyage of discovery of our own and our partner's personality. We felt we could weather the unpleasant discoveries—and indeed, there proved to be some—provided we cared enough for each other to openly deal with and resolve them when they happened. We would try to relate to each other in ways that would never find us in the position of a couple we knew: After twenty years of marriage and one inch away from divorce, the husband cried out when he saw the pancakes on the breakfast table, "All you ever give me are thin pancakes. You never once made me the thick pancakes I like, and you know how I hate thin pancakes." The wife was puzzled. She had been making pancakes for her husband for twenty years. True, the pancakes were always thin. But this was the first time in twenty years her husband had told her he preferred thick ones instead.

7 Practicing the Art of Creative Commitment

After our remarriage shock subsided, Pat and I were to experience many other surprises as we settled "up" to married life. In the past, marriage has been described as the time for settling "down." Settling down implies restricting personal growth, limiting individual possibilities. Old-style marriage was the way one proved oneself a socially accepted adult. Each partner assumed preordained marital roles and obligations: king-of-the-Castle husband who was also the provider and responsible father; deferential wife who was also the nest builder, sex receptacle, and mother. They pledged togetherness till the end of time even though time might erode all dreams, hopes, and expectations.

No, Pat and I had no intention of settling "down" to married life. We, along with millions of other divorced people, are fortunate to be living in a world that allows men and women to explore different options for themselves. We can take as our option what Buddha recommended twenty-five hundred years ago as the pathway to an enriching life:

"Do not believe in what you have heard; do not believe in traditions because they have been handed down for many generations; do not believe anything because it is rumored and spoken of by many; do not believe merely because the written statement of some old sage is produced; do not believe in conjecture; do not believe in that as truth to which you have become attached by habit; do not believe in the authority of your elders.

"After observation and analysis, when it agrees with reason and it is conducive to the good and benefit of one and all, then accept it and live up to it."

Fine words, but how could Pat and I put them into practice? It is one thing to want to relate in new ways, but it is something else to implement those brave ideals every day. Our only guidelines proved to be ourselves and our trust in our capacity to create the new conditions that would enhance our lives. The freedom to do new things is not an unmixed blessing. With freedom comes fear—the fear of taking responsibility and the fear that we might make a shambles of our life together. Old-style marriage at least guarantees safety; the husband and wife know their places. Responsibilities are set by society rather than by self-definition. There is undeniable comfort in saying to oneself, "This is the way the world is and it won't ever change, thank heavens." But for more and more not-so-recently divorced people, old-style marriage is inconceivable. Why head for the fire when one has jumped out of the frying pan? The choice for us is either to attempt to create new forms of intimacy based on mutual respect or to consider intimacy impossible to attain; either to risk moving into the creative-commitment stage or to remain in the selective-distancing stage of learning to love again. The price we pay for moving into the creative-commitment stage is fear and anxiety, for these are the normal consequences of making such a fundamental decision. Stretching ourselves one inch farther than we think we can stretch does not guarantee we will achieve that additional inch. But *not* stretching guarantees we won't. This is the difference between growth and stagnation.

Half of all remarriages end in divorce. Many men and women do not automatically learn from their past experience. Would Pat and I be any different? The fact that I was a professional psychological counselor did not mean that my chance for establishing a lasting love relationship was any better than that 50 percent breakup figure indicates. To the contrary, my professionalism was a negative rather than a positive factor. Some of the most traumatic, painful divorces are experienced by professional men and women such as myself—the psychiatrists, psychologists, counselors, and social workers. And many of their remarriages end the same way. There is a virus of "superiority" which can infect people like me. Because we help others, we may feel we are more competent than other people to deal with our own marital difficulties. Smugness can blind us to the ways we relate to our spouses. Our outrageously inflated professional self-images clash against the everyday reality of our own marriages turning sour. This certainly happened to me in my own divorce, which I described in *Creative Divorce*. That humbling experience shocked me into becoming more of a human being, but there was no certainty that I would relate to Pat differently in our new marriage. I was scared. But fear can be a sign of growing up.

Pat had established her own hard-earned sense of identity, but also felt fear and uncertainty about the future. When I showed her the previous paragraph, she said, "These were my feelings, too, Mel. We had lived together for almost a year, but did we *really* know that much about each other? Had we been kidding ourselves by being on our best behavior in our living-together arrangement so that the worst would now happen? In the early weeks of our marriage I always had the urge to run to the mirror and see if that person in the mirror had changed for the worse. I had the security of a piece of paper, but I also had the doubt that it would only take time before you would really know me and I you, with the result that we would grow tired of each other. I thought at first I could solve my dilemma by buying a house, which we did a few months after we married. But I was surprised to find out that the house had nothing to do with cementing our relationship. It was the day by day way in which we communicated with each other that had to build up the security I wanted. So I also had to play it by ear."

TWO-GETHERNESS IN PLACE OF TOGETHERNESS

A curious thing frequently happens when people remarry. Somehow the marriage ritual, the rings, the legal piece of paper, all work like black magic on two people who have previously experienced love in a living-together arrangement or a long dating period. Two people, who saw each other as separate individuals before the marriage and were attracted by the uniqueness of each other's personality, now try to change each other into their own images of personal need. This happens to well-meaning, intelligent people—the people who are alert to the pitfalls of old-style marriage, the people who have read books and discussed the implications of intimacy with each other before marriage. Pat and I considered ourselves to be such people and yet we too began to see the black magic working in the early months of our remarriage.

It began with our different food habits. After we married, the dinner meals seemed to get bigger and bigger. Each night, at 6 P.M., it would be staring me in the face. If it wasn't pasta, cheese, and garlic bread or corned beef and cabbage, it was Swedish meatballs and strawberry shortcake dessert. I could see Pat anticipate my pleasure as we sat down and prepared to eat. I would eat only small amounts, while Pat cleaned her plate of the last crumb. "Eat more, don't you like my food?" Pat would ask me; and I would reply that the food was marvelous but I was not very hungry. She accepted that explanation at the beginning, but when I continued to be "not hungry" almost every day of the first two months of our marriage, resentment and hostility began to flash in her eyes. Every night I told her the dinner was marvelous, and then ate little of it. Our dinner periods became times of irritation rather than pleasure. Neither of us dared to start a discussion of what was happening between us. We pretended nothing was wrong.

What was going on here? We weren't aware of the source of the difficulty at the time. I reacted to Pat's tensions with silent resentment and uneasiness. Suddenly our brave words about being open and sharing what we felt came back to accuse me. What we had said we were going to do and what we were doing were two entirely different things. Had marriage changed us that much? In our living-together arrangement this problem of sharing who we were never arose in this form; we had concentrated primarily on consolidating our secure single-person identities. Marriage drew us closer as an interdependent couple. . . . But, of course, that was the answer. As the bond of intimacy grows stronger between two people, so does their capacity to hurt or be hurt by each other. Vulnerability coexists with love. There were many good things happening in the early months of our marriage that had already given the lie to the idea that a new relationship must repeat old ways of relating. Marriage had enhanced rather than diminished our sexual delight in each other. And Pat and I felt increasingly comfortable in and supportive of each other's feelings and actions. I could share my hopes and my frustrations about my new career as a divorce adjustment counselor and I found her concerned suggestions extremely helpful; she wanted to return to school and get a degree in psychology and I reinforced her desire for a career without feeling competitive or threatened. In addition we were practicing a degree of openness with each other that we had never done in previous relationships and we had found that it had a positive rather than a negative effect on our relationship.

But neither of us applied this knowledge to our dinner-table difficulties. I had sensed that the six o'clock ritual of serving large dinners was in some way terribly important to Pat. I felt that if I told her how I really felt it would hurt her, so I kept silent. I felt that if I hurt her, she would hurt me by withdrawing her love from me. But our silences were increasing rather than diminishing the tension between us. My fear of losing Pat's love was actually causing the loss of that love. The fact that we had grown more deeply in love after our marriage had increased our capacity to hurt or be hurt by each other.

I was to find out that Pat's fear of losing my love was equal to my fear of losing hers. One night, when I had pushed a giant plate of spaghetti away from me, Pat finally exploded: "You just don't like my food, why don't you say so? Your eating habits are rotten!" At that moment I realized that in some way unknown to me, I had threatened her. My immediate inclination was to tell her to go to hell, but instead I concentrated on the fear that I felt was at the bottom of her explosion. I asked her why she put what seemed to me to be excessive importance on my eating everything on my plate. I told her I had come from a family in which we ate on the run at no set time. My father, because of his work, was rarely home for dinner and it made no difference how much of any dinner I ate. I liked some, but not all of Pat's food, and I certainly did not share her passion for butter. Besides, long before I met her I had conditioned myself to eating small portions of all foods. I have a tendency to gain weight if I even look at a tasty dish. And while Pat might be hungry at six o'clock every night, I was not; frequently I preferred eating earlier or later.

After I explained my actions and asked her why she felt I had to react to dinner in the same way she did, the answer came: love me, love my food. For Pat, as for many women, an elaborate dinner is an act of love. "I want to do nice things for the person I love," Pat said. "When I married you I thought, gee we are really going to make it, especially with the food, because you're Jewish and Jewish people like to eat. My mother really could cook up a storm for my father, my older sister, and me every night. After a hard day's work on the Golden Gate Bridge, Dad would come home and expect a giant dinner on the table at six o'clock sharp every night. Dinner was a happy get-together time and we were expected to eat everything put before us. But everything was so good, that was no problem. And Mom would always beam when Dad praised her cooking, which he always did. It always seemed to me that it was his way of telling her he loved her. She always used the best ingredients, lots of butter—just like I do. But here you are not giving a damn about all the work I go through. I plan things and shop and spend hours in the kitchen and all you do is push the plate away from you and I don't even get a thank you. I've been feeling there must be something wrong with me if you don't like my cooking. Maybe you're growing tired of me; maybe I've done something that has turned you off. I love you so much, but I feel I'm losing your love and I feel so miserable!''

At long last we had raised for discussion what was at the heart of our difficulty in relating to each other. Instead of dropping the subject, we spent much time in the next few days exploring it. Both of us realized it was much more than a matter of eating habits. At the base of the problem was a terrible fear of losing each other's love. To become unloved by the person you care for so deeply is too painful a condition to contemplate or expose. Better to deny the fear and accept the silent anger rather than touch the terror inside that screams that our loved one might disappear! No matter how old a person is, the need for love is so basic that the threat of its disappearance takes each of us back to the ways we were conditioned to love as children. We are never more than one step away from being children again *in our feelings* when we are faced with this apparent threat.

At the dinner table Pat and I had been frightening each other. Our love created an "as if" emotional connection with the people we cared for most deeply as children—our parents. At an unconscious level it is "as if" the person we love *is* our parents and each of us *is* the vulnerable child dependent on pleasing our parents to maintain or win their love. Pat felt she had to show me the love she knew from her childhood. The six o'clock giant dinner of the kind of food she and her parents had enormously enjoyed. We had been viewing love the way children view love, as a precious possession that is won or maintained at the expense of our individuality. This is the rock on which most intimate love relationships founder sooner or later. A dinner estrangement can, over the months and years, mount up to towering resentments over different opinions on money, sex, children, in-laws, and values, unless the fundamental fear of becoming unloved is understood and dealt with early in a marriage. Otherwise, the second, third, or fourth remarriage will be a carbon copy of the first. Four years after that dinner incident happened, I ran across some eloquent comments on loving that Erich Fromm had written:

"Can one *have* love? If we could, love would need to be a thing, a substance that one can have, own, possess. The truth is there is no such thing as 'love.' . . . In reality, there exists only the *act of loving*. To love is a productive activity. It implies caring for, knowing, responding, affirming, enjoying: the person, the tree, the painting, the idea. It means bringing to life, increasing his/her/its aliveness. It is a process, self-renewing and self-increasing. . . .

During courtship neither person is yet sure of the other, but each tries to win the other. Both are alive, attractive, interesting, even beautiful—inasmuch as aliveness always makes a face beautiful. Neither yet *has* the other; hence each one's energy is directed to *being*, i.e., to giving to and stimulating the other. With the act of marriage the situation frequently changes fundamentally. The marriage contract gives each partner the exclusive possession of the other's body, feelings, and care. Nobody has to be won over any more, because love has become something one *has*, a property. . . . What they do not see is that they are no longer the same people they were when they were in love with each other; that the error that one can *have* love has led them to cease loving. . . . The difficulty does not lie in marriage, but in the possessive, existential structure of both partners. . . .*

Old ways of relating die hard. Our awareness of what was happening in our relationship had to be expanded and communicated to each other as we lived each day of our marriage. We had to alert ourselves to our tendency to treat the other person as a possession and love as a reward and punishment system. By focusing on "what dunnit" rather than "who dunnit," we became able to relax and tolerate each other's dinner habits. We are "two-gether" instead of "together" at the dinner table and we have carried over that

---

*Erich Fromm, *To Have or to Be?* New York: Harper & Row, 1976, pp. 44-46.

approach to other areas of our lives. We no longer swallow each other up as the dessert of each evening meal.

THE FEAR BEHIND MARITAL ANGER

I told my colleague, Dr. Seymour Boorstein, about our dinner-table difficulties. I knew he was doing unique and significant work on the ways anger and fear interfere with, and eventually destroy, potentially fine marital relationships. I hope his recommendations for how married men and women can correct tendencies to self-destruct relationships will be as helpful to you as they were to Pat and me:

"Anger is usually the vehicle by which a marriage gets destroyed. Anger usually involves hurting and it usually involves some power struggle. Whenever people are struggling for power, it is hard for love to coexist. To the degree that we are looking for power, to that degree we are less able to love. I don't mean by "power" the strength within oneself. I mean power as a mode of relating to other people, as it relates to getting others in your control, manipulating them, getting them to do your bidding.

"Whenever couples quarrel over money, children, friends, relatives, sex, or personal habits, I would try to look for the common denominator underlying the quarrel. That common denominator seems to be looking for power to cope with the underlying feelings of fear or weakness. A person has a need to feel economically secure. If this need is not fulfilled he or she gets angry in an attempt to overcome the feeling of insecurity. But under the anger is fear. Most often people are not aware of this fear at all. It occurs so quickly and usually unconsciously. It stems from a need (in this case the need for economic security) and that need not being fulfilled. However, a person is ordinarily only aware of the fact that he or she is angry, and the fear step is usually skipped over completely. Why? Because it feels more comfortable for most people to be angry than to be frightened.

"I think you can see this clearly in people who have gone to prison for doing very hurting things. They are most frightened of letting themselves know how frightened they are. So they erect this entire superstructure of anger as a way of coping with the fear. It is an aggressive way of coping to deny the fear. I remember one man in prison who stated that he had to stand and shoot it out with the police because if he turned and ran he would be so frightened he would turn into nothing.

"People, if they were not frightened, would be primarily loving. It is their fears that cause them to do things which prevent loving relationships. To the degree that we are frightened, to that degree do we live our lives less lovingly. Since most of us are not capable of that kind of selfless love that is ascribed to saints, we usually wind up being selfish. There are many levels of love. The highest level, if we could be loving to each other as the saints would, is where we would be loving just for the sheer pleasure of loving the other person without even expecting anything back: If it was returned—that's fine; if it wasn't, that would not matter because the pleasure would come in giving one's love. However, our selfishness causes us to start hurting our spouses or mates when our need for being loved seems to be under attack. Our fear system then sets in motion, and the fear is covered over and is expressed as anger. It springs from the embedded feeling that if my spouse doesn't want to gratify me, it means my spouse doesn't care for me, doesn't love me and maybe will leave me—and I will be alone and abandoned just like a helpless child. For example, if you ask the question of someone in a miserable marriage where he or she feels unloved, 'What if you are unloved, so what? After all, aren't there others in this world you can relate lovingly to?' you will not get a mature answer. Instead, the response is like that of a little child who is frightened, rather than a reaction in terms of his or her adult capacity to go out and make other relationships. It is like feeling one is not getting what is needed to survive. The feeling of being unloved by one's spouse can feel as if one's breathing is about to be stopped. The fear is the not unrealistic childhood fear that without love one would die.

"It has become quite fashionable today to teach and encourage people to externally express their anger as a way of resolving marital disputes, such as 'fighting fair' instead of 'fighting dirty.' This idea assumes that getting feelings out in the open and confronting each other directly is the only alternative to the harmful suppression of anger; letting anger silently boil inside oneself indeed causes physical and emotional damage. However, I believe there is a more constructive alternative available for married people. I think it is better to fight fair than to fight dirty. It is better to fight a little dirty than not to fight at all and let your unexpressed anger totally demolish you. But I think that a way even better than fighting fair would be getting to the real issues behind the fighting. Instead of fighting fair, why fight at all? . . . or fight nominally and not feed the anger. For contrary to the notion that one feels better for having gotten it off one's chest, the expression of anger often leaves one feeling drained and demoralized. I believe that the alternative to both the suppression or excessive external expression of anger is to have couples identify and explore the nature of their fears that give rise to their anger at each other in the first place. Then they can focus their energy on dealing with these fears directly. When they get insight into these fears and can share and discuss them openly with each other, then anger pretty much dissolves and they are capable of constructively resolving their problems.''

RENEWING THE RELATIONSHIP THROUGH MUTUAL UNDERSTANDING

A creative commitment is an ongoing process rather than a possession like a house or a car. Each person must be sensitive to what is happening in the relationship while it is happening. For the not-so-recently divorced men and women who remarry, the memory bank of past remembered hurts is great. We are quick to push the button of those ''I-have-been-here-before'' feelings whenever our spouse appears inattentive to our needs or seems to be uncaring and unloving. Differences in any commitment, creative or otherwise, inevitably arise. It is the way two people in a marriage deal with abrasions that will determine the duration and quality of the relationship. Dr. Boorstein's guidelines for dealing with angry marital confrontations can help improve the quality of the relationship. The best time to try this new approach is after your next fight, after both of you have cooled down, and there is some goodwill between you. You can't very well begin to use the guidelines in the middle of a battle because the struggle for power blocks understanding of what is going on. Here are Dr. Boorstein's guidelines:

□ *Neither push away the anger nor indulge in it. Notice it instead.*

When both of you notice the anger you will realize that you derive *pleasure* from being angry with each other. Your pleasure creates a tendency to continue the use of fighting to resolve new difficulties. The pleasure you get from fighting perpetuates angry ways of relating. It is easy to get hooked on the pleasure of righteous indignation, the pleasure of punching back, the pleasure of revenge, the pleasure of proving oneself right. Anger affords the pleasure of immediate release of tension, no matter what the consequences; it is like scratching an itch—even if it hurts you still want to tear at it. The fear of losing face in a fight is another reason why spouses perpetuate the anger they are feeling toward each other. The anger masks the fear of having the person you love think badly of you, a fear that is frequently too painful for you to acknowledge. In addition, losing face in front of third parties (children, friends, etc.) can be particularly painful because our self-esteem feels lessened or demolished. One defends against the fears relating to the loss of self-esteem by anger. To many people, "losing" a fight is a defective way, but a way nonetheless, of protecting oneself against feelings of worthlessness. Acknowledge to yourselves that those kinds of stakes exist in perpetuating angry disputes and that you must deal with and give them up in order to reach the root causes of the fighting.

□   *Shift gears by focusing on the fears behind the anger.*

Perhaps you and your spouse hollered at each other because you scared each other in some way. Behind the barrage of anger that your spouse directs at you, you will find a scared person who needs reassurance, not a bloodletting argument.

Suppose a woman wants to buy an expensive house. Her

husband says: "I'm furious at you for wanting to buy that horribly expensive place; we could never afford it!" Instead of lashing back with equal anger, the wife could say: "I must have done something to frighten you, but that was not my intention. What could you be afraid of?" The husband is not usually aware that he is frightened since he is concentrating on his anger at her. But when his attention is directed toward his fears, and he is allowed to identify and share them with her, their need to continue the fight and indulge in their anger disappears since it is no longer relevant. This approach assumes that both are people of goodwill, and that in the moment that they lash out at each other they still keep in mind their desire to make the relationship work. If the husband tunes into his fear and asks himself "How did I get frightened?" and tells his wife: "Look, you frightened me because I felt you were trying to destroy me through your selfishness. I thought that if we bought that house we wouldn't have money left for food and we would starve. When I was a child my father was always worried about whether or not he could pay the next month's rent, and here I feel that you were placing me in that same position. It is like you don't love me but loved the house you wanted instead. Otherwise, you would agree with me and forget the house."

The wife can tell him that she wants the house *because* she loves and cares for him. She thought the new place would offer them more space and comfort than they had. She can share with him the feeling that his anger made her feel he hated her and she was ready to scream and accuse him of selfishness.

Instead of attacking each other with righteous indignation, the couple could constructively consider the issues. What are their real and projected assets and income? Do both of them agree that the new house would be a more desirable place to live? What are the real risks involved in buying the new place? (not the risk of starvation as the husband imagined). Insight becomes a better substitute for anger since it eliminates the fog of blind rage that obscures the possibility of realistic decision-making and reasonable compromises.

□   *How you act in an angry situation determines the outcome of the situation.*

It takes two to fight. If one person won't fight, there can't be a fight. You have the choice either to feel threatened by your spouse and fight, or to understand why you feel threatened and therefore have no need to fight. If you feel angry, you can say: "Yes, I got angry—okay, now what's behind it and how can I resolve it?" That means neither holding on to the anger nor putting yourself down for it, because that also feeds the anger in a negative way. Ask yourself: "How did I get frightened?" "Why did I scream at my spouse?" "How did I scare my spouse?" "How did my spouse scare me?"

The answers to these questions will be found in your fear that you are being rejected as unloved and unlovable. Bringing these fears to the surface and opening them up to mutual examination can prevent them from controlling your life. When you take this this kind of initiative you offer your spouse the opportunity to respond in kind. The process of doing so diminishes the need for either of you to ride your rage against the other any further.

□   *Allow yourself and your spouse a trial period in which to practice this alternative approach to fighting.*

New ways of relating don't just happen overnight. They clash against old habits and emerge in bits and pieces, haltingly, awkwardly, clumsily, and self-consciously at first. But new ways can become a part of yourself and no longer require conscious effort. For this approach to be effective, you have to give up the pleasure derived from feeling angry in a fight and let your reason take over, if only for a moment. Otherwise you will be sitting on the anger and not getting to the fear—the fear that your spouse is non-caring and doesn't love you. Since nobody is perfect and you have never used this approach before, it is too much to expect at first that you or your mate will be able to allow your reason to take over even for an instant while the two of you are fighting. It's like when two dogs meet—the first one growls and the second one feels threatened and he has to growl back because he feels he is under attack. Therefore, in the beginning, practice this new approach *after* the fight, maybe a few days later when the hurt has diminished. Try then to reconstruct what happened and get in touch with the ways you scared each other.

At the beginning there will be a long delay between the anger and getting to the fear behind it and you may have to reconstruct what happened in many fights. But as both of you get better at it, the time between the fight and looking at the fear that caused the fight will get shorter, and eventually you will be able to use your anger as a cue even while the fight is going on. Each of you will be able to say: "Uh-huh—I got scared right now. How did I get scared?" and work with your fear on the spot. When you recognize that the threat you perceive coming from your partner is an imagined or an unrealistic threat—and your partner recognizes that he or she has interpreted your actions the same way—the anger between you will dissolve. The need for both of you to get angry will be eliminated.

How both of you explore and communicate your observations about how you were frightened, what you were frightened of, and why you were frightened is crucial. It is not what you say to each other so much as *how* you say it. You can say almost anything, good or bad, but the way you say it can either end the fight before it starts or intensify the anger between the two of you. If you say to your spouse, "I must have frightened you" in a way that implies that he or she is a poor, weak, little thing, your put-down will invite angry retaliation. But if you say the same words with empathy and are mindful of where the other person is, your words will have a positive effect.

This takes some doing in the beginning if your spouse is angrily attacking you at the time. You might become angry in return because that is what you always did in the past. But you can try to catch yourself in the midst of your own anger and shift your attention to your fear and the reasons behind it and then communicate your findings to your spouse. Both of you will then begin to shift your energies from indulging in your anger to constructively resolving the real issues in the dispute. Be patient with each other and with yourself. It won't always work in the beginning, but repeated practice may provide more gratifying results than either of you ever anticipated. Two people who are basically loving toward each other, who experience goodwill and caring about each other's welfare and growth, can transform angry old habits into more positive new ways of relating to each other.

SEX AND LOVE: MAKING THE CONNECTION

In a creative commitment, sex is simply the unself-conscious, earthy affirmation of the loving connection between two people.

Easier said than done! I have found more confusion, unrealistic expectations, misunderstandings, vulnerability, disillusionment, and fear expressed by the men and women attending my Learning to Love Again Seminars when they discuss how sex fits into their lives than when they discuss any other subject. The gap between sex and love in their lives is sizable indeed. This doesn't surprise me, since it took me half a lifetime before I began to bridge that gap myself. The sexual dilemma people find themselves in has nothing to do with their intelligence or intellect. In fact, the most highly intellectual people often evidence the greatest blind spots. Why should this be so? After all, hasn't there been a "sexual revolution" in this country in the past decade? Isn't it true that sex is no longer the dirty little secret people were afraid to talk about? Isn't premarital sex the norm rather than the exception? Aren't we saturated with sex discussions, sex workshops, and "how-to-do-it" sex books? This is all true—and all to the good, as far as I'm concerned. The more information and open discussion about so vital a part of people's lives, the better. For our society to acknowledge that sex is a healthy and joyous expression of who we are as human beings, rather than a shameful animal activity, is a giant step forward. However, it is one thing to take sex out of the closet into the daylight where it belongs. It is quite another to see sex as an answer to all our problems. This is the illusion on which so many potential creative commitments founder. Before sex can assume its appropriate role in a creative commitment, reality has to replace illusion. Most people believe that a sophisiticated knowledge of sex is widespread in our country today. The reality is that we are only at the beginning point in that understanding. The San Francisco Sex Information Service, which answers thousands of phone-call questions that typical, normal Americans ask about their personal lives reveals the reality of sex as it is practiced by most Americans today.

When I asked a Sex Information Service director, Toni Ayres, about the nature of these calls, she told me today's adults (yes, even the generation in their late teens and twenties!) have grown up believing in a grab bag of old wives' and husbands' tales, stereotyped sex roles, and mutual misunderstandings. Their misperception can't be changed overnight but it can be changed. The fact that so many people call Sex Information Service—as many women as men—indicates their willingness to seek answers, which is the first step toward positive sexual relationships. But factual knowledge is *only* a first step, although its importance is frequently overlooked. Most not-so-recently divorced people have had considerable sexual experience if they are in the second and third stages of learning to love again. And yet they frequently don't have much factual information. Don't be surprised if you don't, too, for I've been in the same boat. It wasn't so long ago that I, in my middle years, was unaware of the great importance of the clitoris as the source of female sexual arousal. Nor was I aware that the entire human body is a sexual instrument, so that touching, feeling, caressing, smelling, tasting, and vocal sounds are of enlivening importance for maximizing sexual pleasure.

In a creative commitment, knowledge of sexual facts and techniques can only supplement an already good sexual relationship. They cannot create that relationship. Masters and Johnson, the famous sex therapists, have indicated that as many as two-thirds of all marital relationships are sexual disaster areas. The main reason for this is not lack of knowledge about sexual facts and techniques, but lack of knowledge that sex is not a possession or power trip, but an expression of a pleasure-giving and pleasure-receiving, loving relationship between two people.

If you are a not-so-recently divorced person who has experienced the second and third stages of learning to love again, you have gone through a learning process that can enable you to experience sex in a creatively committed way. The clue that you are ready to reexamine and reevaluate your sexual attitudes and actions resides in the disillusion, dissatisfaction, or depression you may be feeling right now about the quality of your sexual life. Now is the time to sort out the meaning of your varied sexual experiences and come to terms with your sexuality and the sexuality of others in a more fulfilling manner. You are ready to do so if you are saying to yourself (as have so many of the women in my Learning to Love Again Seminars), "Every sexual experience I've had where my horniness was the only reason for hopping into bed was bad; I have to like the person; I have to feel a great warmth toward him; I have to be turned on to a lot more than just the act." This is no different from what many men are saying. As one man eloquently put it, "I like to go all night and I like the romance. I know that I appreciate sex and enjoy sex as a woman would. For me, I've come to understand that going to bed with somebody isn't just having a bang-bang and good-bye. It is having someone hold me, caress and kiss and touch me, which makes me feel I'm wanted.''

When not-so-recently divorced men and women realize that they want more from sex than release of physical tension after they have lived through the second and third learning to love again stages, new and more satisfying sexual experiences become possible.

Jeff's story is a dramatic example of what can happen when you see with a new perspective the old sexual assumptions you may have been living. Jeff is a thirty-seven-year-old photographic equipment salesman, divorced four years, and has had a wide variety of sexual experiences:

"That first year after my divorce I discovered sex was great. That was good to know since my wife once told me that having sex with me was like being assaulted with a dead weapon. But I found out it was just that we had not been right for each other. I've had lots of affairs, because I was so starved for sex in my marriage, and I thought good sexual relationships would cure all my problems. What a laugh! When you're deprived, you think you are like a man in a desert looking for an oasis. But after you've had your fill you take it for granted and want something more than sexual acrobatics. I've become tired of the performance trip I've been putting on my penis and I've stopped going to the single-bar meat markets.

"My God, this is a cock-oriented society. Such stupid emphasis on performance. Why does everything have to be judged by erections, staying power, and orgasms? What about warmth, sensitivity, and tenderness? Touching, tasting, smelling, cuddling, looking, holding, talking . . . doesn't this count at all? Well I've learned it does. I no longer worry about whether or not I will have an erection or a premature ejaculation if I'm with a woman I like very much. And oh how I used to worry about that!

"I'm now involved in a different kind of relationship with a woman. The flow of our relationship now determines what happens to me sexually. I don't press; I don't worry; and if I'm not "potent," it's no big deal any more. The evening is "successful" for all the good things going on between the two of us, whether or not the earth moves. And you know what? My sexual potency has actually improved as a result of not worrying about it all the time. That has really surprised and delighted me. . . . I have discovered there are a lot of women around today who have bought the performance trip. I've dumped it—but they've bought it. I steer clear of them because I think it's kind of sad that they are taking on themselves the worst of men's hang-ups. They have the crazy idea that sex means only talking in four letter words like men and demanding sustained erections and multiple orgasms exploding like bombs inside. Some of them call it "sport-fucking!" They compare notes about who the best studs are and circulate the studs as if the men were pieces of meat. Sure men have done that to women. But men and women like that are damned unhappy people. I recently met a lovely woman whom I could talk to about this and she said that women had always had performance hang-ups of their own.

"She said she used to feel not very confident about her ability to perform the way a sexpot should perform, and that maybe she wasn't doing things right or exciting enough. But now, she tells me, she can just be herself, not super-sexy all the time. That sounds great to me. I am beginning to think I can be me too—that I have something more to offer than a penis—like sensitivity, intelligence, humor, and love, for instance.

What Jeff is learning is what Jill and Ned are experiencing in the fourth year of their marriage. It is the second marriage for Jill and the third for Ned. Both are in their mid-forties and this is what they have learned:

"With my first husband it was sex and no closeness," Jill said. "So then I didn't want sex. The way I feel about a good relationship with a man is I like the closeness of it, and if the closeness develops into sex that's marvelous. First comes the closeness and the communication, that's the way it's been between Ned and me, and the turn-ons are so much greater. I think sex begins in the kitchen and living room. It's how we act toward each other in all aspects of our lives together. Sex is just part of the whole thing; I don't separate it out."

While Jill was talking, Ned was nodding in agreement. "I feel our relationship is the whole thing," he then said. "As a result, the sex is much more gratifying. It is in many ways a culmination of what we're doing minute by minute. It's a pretty good barometer of how close we are together. When we were first married I went through a few months of fear about how good she would think my performance was and would that be a problem. It was like my first and second wives were in the bedroom with us still criticizing my performance the way they used to! Then something wonderful happened. One night Jill was feeling sexier than I was. I had had a grueling day at the office, so when she snuggled up to me and became amorous in bed I struggled to get an erection but wasn't up to it, if you will forgive the pun. So I said to Jill, 'I'm sorry.' She looked at me with love and tenderness and said: 'But why are you sorry? What are you trying to prove? I love your just being close to me and talking to me and caring for me in the way you touch me and kiss me. I love you for being you, not because you can get an erection and orgasm inside me one hundred percent of the time.' From that night on my performance fears disappeared. Jill was right. I did not have to prove anything. I just have to be me. That's true of Jill also. The more secure we've become with each other, the easier it all is. And that's because we feel more secure about ourselves. We don't need to prove through sex that we're valuable people. All we have to do is to enjoy the sex we have together.''

The men and women who are creatively committed to each other learn in the process of living together that sex is a psychological barometer of their relationship. The intensity and frequency of their turn-ons and turn-offs are determined by the extent to which the underlying basis of their relationship is a loving and trusting one rather than a selfish, controlling, or domineering one. When a relationship sours, sex becomes an obsessive concern: All of the deficiencies in the relationship turn into complaints about frigidity, impotency, absence of orgasmic satisfaction, premature ejaculation, and I've-got-a-headache excuses.

In a creative commitment, however, sex is one of many forms in which the satisfying nature of your relationship is celebrated. The sexual act becomes a statement of mutual love as physical delight. There is no need under such circumstances to be obsessively concerned about sex, since there are no problems in relating to each other to be obsessively concerned about.

8 But What About the Children?

"I didn't marry my wife, I married a crowd," said Phil, a recently remarried man. "There are my three sons, who give me the silent treatment when they see me every other weekend, *and* the twin ten-year-old daughters of my new wife, Carolyn, who frankly are often a pain in the ass, *and* my new in-laws, who cold-shoulder me, *and* Carolyn's ex-husband, who spoils the twins rotten when he sees them, *and* my ex-wife, who is still bad-mouthing me to my kids, *and* the Bank of America's Credit and Loan Department. The guy who said two can live as cheaply as one ought to be shot!"

Welcome to the club, Phil. You have become, along with Pat and me, a member of a vast—and neglected—group in our society, known as stepparents.

In the United States today there are twenty-five million

husbands and wives who are stepfathers and stepmothers. Fifteen million children under eighteen live in step families, and well over half a million men and women, and their children, swell our ranks every year. Phil was not aware of these statistics any more than I was when I remarried four years ago. Nor would they have made any difference in Phil's or my decision to remarry if we had known them.

In a creative commitment two people marry each other out of strength rather than weakness: They have built up within themselves secure single-person identities that enable them to risk intimacy again. They are secure in the knowledge that they have the capacity to cope effectively with the unexpected, the problems, the crises that may arise in their committed relationship. They can't predict what will happen in their future, but they know that the way they relate to each other is the central factor that will enable them to weather successfully whatever storms may arise. Their intelligence, their sharing, their empathy, their flexibility, their compassion, their intimacy, their maturity will carry them through to a safe harbor. They have learned through their experience in relating to each other that a creative commitment does not take place overnight: Moving through the successive stages of learning to love again took time and each person's right to proceed at his or her own pace had to be respected. Neither will the creation of a fulfilling new set of family relationships take place overnight.

The lessons learned before remarriage are the lessons that can and must be applied to the challenge of the new family structure in which you and your new spouse will be involved. Otherwise, you and your spouse will relive old-style marriage rather than a creative commitment, and the marriage will end in mutual resentments, anger, and bitterness. The high rate of divorce for the remarried is no accident. The major reason for it is the inability of many couples to cope constructively with precisely the kinds of problems Phil complained about—particularly problems dealing with the children.

Most remarriages involve new relationships with strangers who suddenly become stepchildren. Phil had two living with him and Carolyn had three who arrived for a visit every other week. When I remarried I became stepparent to Pat's two daughters, Vickie, who was sixteen and was to live with us, and Karen, who had recently married. Pat had two new stepdaughters—my children, Julie and Nora, who were in college and living in other cities.

When you remarry, you think of yourself as a stepparent but forget that your children are seen as stepchildren by your new spouse. When that happens, you create a double standard. For then you send out signals to each other that demand, "Love my children as I love them, but allow me not to love your children the way you love them." The implied or spoken demand of "If you really loved me you would love my children as much as I love them" injects a lethal dose of old-style marriage into a creative commitment. Possessiveness, anxiety, excessive jealousy, insecurity, self-centeredness, and lack of self-esteem are the seed beds in which that demand flourishes. The way you and your spouse deal with the stepparenting problems inherent in a remarriage is a good test of whether or not you are living an old-style marriage or a creative commitment. If not dealt with appropriately, the difficulties you experience with your children and your stepchildren can become the greatest obstacle to making your remarriage work, even if both of you have agreed to marry for creatively committed reasons.

It is not too difficult to understand why this should be so. Think back to your own childhood: Did you ever feel that your parents were giving you enough of the love, affection, and attention you felt you deserved? Did you ever fantasize that they were not your "real parents," that your real parents were probably a king and queen who would someday claim you so that you would live happily ever after? Did you ever feel angry when your parents broke promises or hurt your feelings? Did you ever retaliate by doing the things you know would disturb them most—not coming home at curfew time, absenting yourself from school, stealing a candy bar at the grocery store, refusing to do the dishes, yelling out four-letter words at the dinner table? Did you ever have mixed feelings of loving and hating your parents at the same time? Did you ever feel guilty because at times you violently disliked your parents—and then feel relieved if they punished you for something you did? Did you ever feel angry that your parents never asked how you felt about a move to a new neighborhood? In other words, didn't you ever feel frightened that you were unlovable and unloved when you were a child?

You would have been an exceptional child if you never experienced these feelings. These normal, painful feelings are as much a part of growing up as the good feelings children experience with their parents. Remembering how you felt as a child will help you understand what your children's and stepchildren's feelings may be when you establish your new family arrangement. This is what is known as having "empathy" with other people—becoming compassionately aware of their feelings. In the new family arrangement, these feelings may be magnified in the children. And if you don't understand what is happening inside their heads, the children may relate to you with hostility, silence, or resentment.

As Phil told me, "I read somewhere that they call the kind of family I have 'the reconstructed family' or 'the blended family.' Well in my house its more like the Civil War period rather than the Reconstruction period—and it's about as blended as oil and water! I love Carolyn very much, but (I hate to say it) I don't like her children. They ignore me by talking only to their mother when we are together. And they play me against their father. 'Why can't we go to the nice places Daddy always takes us?' This is what I hear every time they return from a visit with their father. It's like they make me into a monster and I feel resentful as hell about it. And my own children—wow!—what a change in them! I thought after my divorce that we had established a better relationship among us than we ever did when I was married to my first wife. We opened up and shared more of ourselves and our feelings about each other. But ever since I remarried four months ago they have become like tight clams and I find it hard to talk to them. I know I feel rotten because Carolyn's twins are getting much more of my time than my own kids, since they are living with me. And maybe my kids feel kind of left out. When my kids visit my new house, they're polite enough to Carolyn, but there's ice between them. And Carolyn doesn't go out of her way to make it any better. None of this is what I bargained for. I thought it would be a fresh start for all of us, that a new family in a new house would bring us all closer together. But instead, it is tearing us apart. Carolyn and I have talked all of this out and we have decided to see a family counselor together to get some help before it is too late. Maybe there's something that Carolyn and I are doing that is creating this mess. If that's the case, we sure want to change whatever it is.''

Phil's situation is by no means as desperate as he may think. The very fact that he and his wife are alert enough to seek out professional help *before* their problems reach the point of no return indicates they are practicing the art of creative commitment. The secure single-person identities they built up during the earlier stages of learning to love again enable them to seek outside professional help without considering it a sign of failure or weakness. Without putting themselves or each other down, they accept the possibility that they may be dealing with their problems inappropriately. They are willing to change their ways of relating to their situation, if such change is warranted. Their future looks bright because they are willing to recognize their problems, discuss them openly, and try to reach a mutual decision to resolve them.

Many men and women who are creatively committed to each other, like Phil and Carolyn, seek out professional help about dealing with their children early in their remarriage before the problems drown them. As Judith, thirty-eight, told me: ''I'd be a fool to do in my new marriage what I did in my first. I never used to say anything when I was climbing the walls about something, because of my first husband's fragile ego. I would think maybe the problem would vanish if I ignored it, but it only got worse in the end. When I once suggested we go to a counselor, he told me I could go but he said he never would because he didn't have any problems. It is different with my new husband, Arnold. I must admit I was kind of scared when I told him that the fights between his kids and mine were causing us to fight each other and it was time to take a look at what we were doing. But he was great about it and even volunteered to set up an appointment with a counselor for both of us.''

I have known many men and women who decided to seek counseling *before* their remarriage because they had reservations about how their children would react in the new family structure. Counseling heightened their awareness about what to expect in the new relationship and enhanced their abilities to cope constructively with the stress and strains that normally arise. Pat and I learned the hard way about the illusions and realities of the so-called blended family. We strongly recommend *premarital* counseling for people planning to remarry if they feel that difficulties with the way the children are relating will significantly affect the stability and quality of their remarriage.

EXPECT THE UNEXPECTED

The family created out of a remarriage is neither a ''reconstructed family'' nor a ''blended family.'' The labels are deceiving. Simply because you have remarried, a reconstruction or blending of new family relationships is not an accomplished fact. The reality is that your remarriage presents you and your spouse with the challenge to create within the new family environment a reconstruction or blending of new relationships with your children and your stepchildren. If you enter into a remarriage believing that the new marital structure in and of itself will solve stressful child-related problems, you will only be creating new difficulties for yourself, your new spouse, and the children.

If you tell your children—and believe it yourself—that you are all going to live happily ever after, that they are going to have a nice new father or mother, and nice new brothers and sisters, you will be heading for trouble. You will find yourself disturbed if your children give your spouse the silent treatment and react uncomfortably with you. Or your children and your spouse's children, so well mannered before the remarriage, may start stealing each other's toys and kicking each other in the shins, much to your dismay.

The labels pinned on remarried people and their children create many of the problems. They give rise to false expectations about how the new family is expected to relate. When remarried men and women are labeled step*parents* and the children are labeled step*sons* and step*daughters*, false expectations are bound to arise.

Adele, a thirty-four-year-old woman, whose father remarried when she was sixteen, says it well: "My father, whom I was living with, held back telling me he was going to remarry until the day before the ceremony. It was like he felt kind of guilty telling me. He said we would now have a real family again and that Ruth, his new wife, would be a fine mother to me. Mother, hell! I hardly knew the woman. I loved my real mother, so how could this stranger be a mother to me? I wanted to see my father happy, so if he wanted to marry Ruth, that was fine for him. But what about me? From the very beginning Ruth came on so damned strong. I felt she was pressing too hard for me to like her—that I was supposed to like her or love her even though I hardly knew her, just because she was my father's new wife.

"I didn't realize when I was sixteen what I do now. I now see she was really a good woman with the best of intentions, but she was so terribly insecure. For example, from the start I could never talk to my father when she was in the room because she did all the talking. Or when my father and I would go out to the backyard alone, she would drop what she was doing and insist on being with us too. After all these years I can still hear her say in that loud voice of hers, 'Oh, wait a minute, let me get my sweater and come outside with you!' I was angry and resentful, but I never said anything to her. There never was enough openness in that remarriage for me to say what I wanted to, like: 'Ruth, you're a stranger to me—stop acting as if you want to become my mother. I'll tolerate you because you came into Dad's life and he's so much happier living with you. I love my father and want him to be happy. However, you and I have to work on our relationship together. I can't instantly like or love somebody my father picks out. I would never want to hurt you, but please be quiet sometimes, stop forcing yourself on me!'

"Looking back, I can see that Ruth thought I would be criticizing her and putting her down if she let me talk with my father alone. She was so wrong. After all, Dad and I shared things in common she couldn't possibly know about or be interested in. I knew my father a lifetime, she knew him a few short years. It is funny I should still feel so angry and resentful after eighteen years when I talk about my stepmother and my father. Because my father made me angry too. He kept pushing Ruth in my face with: "Isn't Ruth great?" "Isn't Ruth a marvelous cook?" "Isn't Ruth intelligent?" It was as if I *had* to love her too just because he loved her. And that made me feel guilty, because I didn't love her, which meant I might be hurting my father's feelings. Wouldn't it have been enough to allow me to learn to like and respect her as a good friend? Or to be free just to tolerate her? After all, Dad and I are two different people, so why should he expect me to feel about her the way he did? This has not soured me on remarriage for myself. I'll be able to handle my stepchildren, if there are any, much better than the way I was handled. I learned what not to do from Ruth and my dad!''

Adele's reflections demonstrate the fallacy of assuming that your love and compassion can transform stepchildren into daughters and sons who will love you as much as your children love you. At best, expect the warmth and affection derived from developing a friendship with them and you will find them enriching your life together instead of turning it into a battlefield.

Another unrealistic expectation concerns money, as Phil has indicated. A recently remarried man named Scott put it this way: ''Sarah has custody of her three boys, my ex-wife has custody of my two girls. Sarah and I thought we would be saving money by marrying. After all, we'd been paying two rents for our two separate apartments. I had been eating alone a lot of the time which meant it cost a hell of a lot more to feed myself rather than in a complete family unit where it would work out a lot cheaper. But when we married we found we needed to rent a house large enough to house everybody, a place to include my kids too when they visited us. Renting a house cost us more than renting two separate apartments. I had forgotten about what inflation has done to house rentals! Food, too, is so expensive these days, so there was no saving money like I anticipated.

''The unexpected things that have happened seem unbe- lievable—like Sarah's kids needing expensive dental care and just recently her ex-husband became unemployed so her child-support payments stopped. At the same time my ex-wife is going to court to try to increase my support payments. Can you beat that!''

People in a creative commitment recognize that fights over money—the lack of it, how to stretch it, how to spend it, how to get more of it—can transform a remarriage into a hell. Nothing is more frightening than the feeling of economic insecurity: It becomes an I-have-been-here-before feeling that can make you act—if you let it—as if you are once again a scared little child without sufficient capabilities to survive. ''Whenever I start getting uptight about money,'' says Fay, thirty-one, ''I'm making a statement about my own feelings of insecurity. . . . It's a signal. . . . It means to me that I'm feeling insecure about something.''

Using Dr. Boorstein's approach to these monetary difficulties can prove helpful in avoiding the battles and coming to terms with the fear behind the anger that arises over monetary squabbles. The constructive approach is to recognize before your remarriage that two may very well not be able to live as cheaply as one, and give careful consideration to budgetary arrangements. Acknowledge that unexpected debts and expenses *will* arise, and establish an understanding that both of you will always discuss and mutually work out the monetary decisions you will be faced with. Allow for role flexibility which may very well mean that instead of one person working in the family, both of you may have to work in critical times. If you feel helpless in the face of budget facts and figures, consult at no cost, or at minimum fee, a Consumers' Credit Counseling Service in your area or a family financial counseling service at your local Family Service Agency.

In a creative commitment, money is no longer a fear-based power struggle. Instead, it may be a problem that can cause intense stress, but it will always be resolved constructively since your relationship with your partner is a loving one. Even if painful retrenchments are the order of the day, they will neither diminish nor destroy the love you experience between you. That will be destroyed only if the two of you choose to destroy it.

SEE THE PERSON IN THE STEPCHILD

If you have already experienced a creative divorce, you have learned to understand and respect your children as separate people. One of the great bonuses of a creative divorce is your increased awareness that your children experienced the divorce *differently* than you experienced it. You learned that although you no longer love your ex-spouse, your children still do and always will. You learned to respect your children's feelings and allowed them to feel free to voice their feelings—angry, resentful, hostile, fearful feelings included—and saw how that cleared the air and drew you closer together rather than farther apart. As a result of this experience, you have built up resources within yourself that can enable you to cope constructively with the *new* children-related problems in your remarriage. Now you need to become aware of what to expect, and what not to expect, of the new relationship with the children in the remarriage.

□ *Expect a temporary change in the relationship between you and your children.*
The relationship you established with your children in a

single-parent household, if you are the custodial parent, was different from the relationship you will establish in your remarried household. Your children, accustomed to one way of life, are now suddenly thrust into a new arrangement which affects their sense of security. *You* see the new arrangement as a promise of happiness, but *they* see it as a threat to their very survival. The children may have very mixed feelings: They like to see their parent happy, because if the parent is happy, they feel they won't be abandoned or orphaned. (When a parent is seen to be perpetually sad, helpless, or complaining all the time, the children fear the parent may die or abandon them.) But the children feel fearful, angry, and resentful that "intruders," a stepparent and stepchildren, are now coming into their lives. "Who are these strangers?" "Will they take my mom's (or dad's) love away from me?" "Will I have to give up my real parent who visits me because I have a stepparent now?" "Why did my parent have to marry again and disrupt my life?" "Doesn't my parent know that I want my two real parents to come back and live together with me, not this stranger, and can't my parent see how angry I am that this hasn't taken place?" "Why do I feel angry at the parent I love so much?" These are the questions that typically run through a child's mind when a parent remarries. Young or older, it makes no difference. I have heard nineteen-year-olds voice the same anxieties as seven-year-olds, in one form or another.

Your children may express their anxieties indirectly for fear of hurting you and being punished. As one fifteen-year-old girl said: "When Mom got remarried I stayed out with my friends and cut classes and never came in for dinner on time. Why did she do this to me?" The connection was there:

"I will hurt Mom, whom I love so dearly, because she has hurt me by getting remarried and giving her new husband the love I should be getting," her actions said.

If you are alert to the possibility of disrupted relationships with your children early in remarriage, the fact that they may happen will not shock you. You can cope with the situation in the same way you did in your single-parent household—by being sensitive to the needs of your children, allowing them to express their hurts directly to you, listening to and correcting their fears and fantasies about the new relationship, and reassuring them that you will never love them less than you do. The same understanding is required of the noncustodial parent.

□ *Don't expect your stepchildren to love you instantly.*

Adele's reflections about her stepparent are useful to keep in mind. Otherwise, when you try to kiss your stepdaughter or stepson, they may turn their faces from you, or when you suggest a family picnic they may prefer staying home. There are a million variations on this theme. The following was told to me by a recently remarried woman: "I thought the kids would all get along well with each other—his and mine. But his boys make my girl cry by calling her 'fatty' and 'tub-tank.' Then my girl runs to me and the boys' father makes the boys apologize. And when I ask his boys what they want for lunch, they say that they are not hungry or that they would rather eat at McDonalds. 'I don't want to eat your food because you took our daddy away from us!' is the message they are giving me."

Your stepchildren may be full of similar anxieties about their parent, who is now your spouse. They may feel that their relationship with their noncustodial parent is now threatened. Your awareness of this possibility may help your new spouse, who may be too close to his or her children to see the situation in clear perspective. Sharing your observations with him or her in a truly helpful, concerned way will help put the relationship on a sound footing. How you share your observations is as important as the observations themselves.

□   *Expect to have confused and mixed feelings about your role as a stepparent.*

When you buy a washing machine, you get instructions about how to operate it. When you remarry, you get the title "stepparent" at the top of a blank page. Your natural tendency is to rely for guidelines on the experience from the family you grew up in and the family of your previous marriage. You hope your new family structure will be the same as your past family structures, the only difference being that the new one will be an improvement on the past. This hope is unrealistic, because the assumption it is based on is unrealistic. As one woman told me, "I realize the differences are greater than the similarities between my family in my first marriage and my family in my remarriage. With my remarriage it was like building a house from scratch: One day it's laying the foundation, next day the slabs, then deciding what lumber you want and how big you want this room or that room, and all the time being flexible enough to modify your ideas if your original plan is unworkable in some respect. Remarriage is a whole new game when it comes to kids."

The title "stepparent" may cause you to build on a shaky foundation, if you let it. It can lead to a belief that you must be the stepchild's substitute for the noncustodial parent and give the child the signal that you indeed *are* the father or mother during that parent's absence. You will be sadly disappointed then when you find that your stepchild will never love you—couldn't possibly love you—in the same way, or as much as, he or she loves the noncustodial, biological parent.

You may also feel guilty for having "failed" in "winning" the love of the child if you equate being a stepparent with being a parent. Just as you had to discard images of Super Mom or Super Dad or Disneyland Daddy or Disneyland Mommy in your creative divorce, so you have to dispense with illusions about being a super or Disneyland stepparent for workable relationships with your stepchildren to develop. Nor can you buy the love of your stepchildren by drowning them in gifts any more than you could with your own children in your divorce. Just being yourself as a sensitive, caring, aware human being will prove to be sufficient.

Don't be surprised if you have mixed feelings about your stepchildren. You may feel distressed because the "vibes" between you and these children are not quite right. You may want to like them very much for your new spouse's sake, thinking it will cement the love between you. However, your dislike or bare tolerance of them because of their personalities may make you feel disloyal to your new spouse.

You may feel torn with guilt every time your children visit you, if they are living with your ex-spouse. Your new spouse's children are living with you in your home and getting the lion's share of your time—and they may not even appreciate it—while your own flesh and blood get only a tiny amount of your time. You may feel apologetic, and your own children may feel resentful, every time you get together. Not only that, every time your children visit, they are a barometer of what is happening in your ex-spouse's home. If your ex-spouse is lonely, bitter, or unhappy, your children may bring these feelings with them when they visit you. They like seeing you happy in your marriage, but they may also feel disturbed and sad because your ex-spouse isn't happy. They may feel torn in their allegiance and believe it would be an act of disloyalty to the parent they are living with if they showed their delight in seeing you. Consequently, they may act resentful or cool or distant when they see you, although they would really like to show their happiness at being with you. Understanding this can help you understand your children's seeming lack of affection toward you and enable you to handle your hurt and angry feelings at the way they are acting.

The question of disciplining stepchildren may also confuse you: Act like a parent? Act as if nothing happened? Leave the discipline to your spouse? Feel your stepchildren won't consider you a nice person if you discipline them? Unless you openly acknowledge your dilemma to your spouse and work out a mutually agreeable way to discipline, trouble will be compounded. If your entire family is allowed to participate in the establishment of clear and reasonable household rules, and if the agreed upon disciplinary procedures are jointly enforced in such a way as to prevent the children from playing off one spouse against the other, then disciplinary problems will prove to be manageable.

THE CREATIVE-COMMITMENT GUIDELINES FOR STEPPARENTING

The process of family adjustment in a creatively committed relationship in which children are involved cannot take place overnight, much as you may want that to happen. Expect the first two years after remarriage to be the time for smoothing out a very bumpy road. Positive results begin to occur consistently, rather than sporadically, in the third year. Using the creative commitment approach in dealing with the children can minimize the anxieties, guilt, and frustrations that are built into the new family environment. Here are the creative commitment guidelines that you can put into practice.

□ *Prepare the way for the new family relationship before your remarriage.*

If you spring the remarriage announcement on the children as a last-minute surprise, they may well give you the kind of reaction Adele gave her parents. Allow sufficient time for the children to absorb the fact you are planning to marry again. Invite them to discuss their fantasies and expectations and anxieties with you. Respect their feelings and clarify the realities. Give them the reassurance they need that you will always love them and that the new household arrangement will allow for a continuance of your love rather than its diminution.

□ *Respect the readiness time of the children to adjust to the new family environment.*

You and your new spouse proceeded at your own pace through the stages of learning to love again to arrive at a creative commitment. Children, too, must be allowed flexibility in arriving at a positive relationship with you and your spouse and each other. If you understand that there are stages of development in your stepchildren's relationship to you, you will find it less difficult to accept the fact that the children may not like you instantly as a stepparent.

- In the first stage, you are the stranger who will be living with them and may "take away" their parents' love for them.
- In the second stage, you are a tolerable acquaintance, part of the furniture of the house, but still warily observed (you still may turn out to be untrustworthy; you may even leave the custodial parent just like their real parent left).
- In the third stage, you are a friend in whom they can place increasing trust.
- In the fourth stage you may become a very good friend—a loved friend in fact. But you will never become a loved parent.

When you understand and respect the stage the children are in in relationship to you at a given time, positive things can happen. I can remember those early months when my stepdaughter, Vickie, sixteen, greeted me with deafening silence when I arrived home from work. Every night was the same: She would refuse to eat dinner with Pat and me, slam the door to her room, and hole herself up there for the rest of the evening. When I recently asked her why she had acted that way, she told me, "I felt you really were nice to me and ready to talk. I wanted you to like me, but at that time I wasn't ready for it. I don't think you could have done more, because I was sheltering myself. I never got the feeling you were trying to get me to like you so that Mom would like you more. I felt I didn't want to come out of my shell yet because I was still hurting a lot. I knew I could come out of it, but I felt more comfortable being by myself in the beginning. As time goes on you begin to know and like a person, but you can't expect that to happen overnight. I really thought then that I might be forced to choose between you and my dad, and that Mom would be giving all of her love to you, so that there would be none left for me. Besides, I thought I would be intruding on you and Mom, so it would be better for me to stay in my room. Of course, none of that happened, and we are good friends now.''

It took three years for Vickie and me to become good friends. Pat laid the groundwork for our friendship when she told Vickie early in our marriage: "Vickie, you will always have me and your father as your parents who love you. Mel is my husband, but he will never be your father. He can become a very good friend to you if you will let that happen. He certainly wants to meet you halfway, so it is up to you to decide what you want.''

Reflecting on what she told Vickie four years ago, Pat said to me, "When I told Vickie that, I could see how relieved she felt. She had been afraid that she would be disloyal to her father if she acknowledged any liking for you. What I said to her seemed to free her from her double bind. Now she could be a warm, loving daughter to her father and also not feel guilty over liking you. It took a long time for that to work out in practice, of course, but it would never have happened at all if Vickie's mixed feelings had not been discussed.''

□   *Create an accepting environment for the children.*

You and your spouse can do much to create a family household in which new relationships can flourish instead of wither. First of all, you can "cool it," don't talk too much, listen a lot to what the stepchildren have to say. Treat them as independent people instead of trying to relate to them as a mother or a father. Stop demanding that they give you the kind of affection they can only give to their real parents. If they don't live with you, give them real choices when they visit you, so that they have the freedom (within the normal rules of your house) to do whatever they want to do, whether it is staying apart from you and playing in a separate room or being together with you on a picnic.

Demonstrate by actions rather than by words or promises that you regard the stepchildren as potential friends. Let them know they can spend as much time as they wish alone with their own parent, your spouse. Leaving your stepchildren alone with their natural parent for an entire day is a test of your self-esteem. But there is nothing to fear; they are not conspiring against you; there is no need to feel jealous over the time your spouse spends with his or her children. Allow the children to see the openness in your relationship with your spouse, which will permit them to be free to express the wider range of their feelings. As one teen-age girl said to her stepfather: "I never used to hear my mom and dad talk and argue and share their feelings. All I can remember was just the silence between them. But you and Mom together are so different. It's great to hear both of you let it out. And there is always laughter at the end of your arguments—it's like you cleared the air and reached some sort of decision on what to do. I like that because I feel I can let out my feelings, too, without being put down."

□   *Be honest with your feelings.*

The new family arrangement can prove to be the largest guilt-manufacturing factory in the world—if you permit it:

□ A stepmother is in bed with the flu while her fifteen-year-old stepdaughter visits for the weekend. When the stepdaughter leaves to return to her mother's home, she hollers into the room, "Good-bye Jo," without saying she hopes her stepmother's health improves. Jo feels hurt and anger—and guilt over feeling angry. She feels like a wicked stepmother because she momentarily dislikes her new husband's daughter, whom she ordinarily likes. In becoming angry at her stepdaughter, she feels as if she has betrayed her spouse.

□ Henry sends his two sons, aged twenty-three and thirty, plane tickets to fly from Chicago to Los Angeles to visit him the day before his remarriage. When they arrive, he intends to tell them he will remarry. Shocked and resentful at having this announcement sprung on them, his children refuse to attend the wedding and return east before it occurs. The father had felt that his children might disapprove of his remarrying, which is why he had kept it a secret until the last moment. Now the father feels additional guilt because his children left without attending the ceremony.

□ Ten-year-old Tommy has called his mother at her office for the fifth day in a row. Each time he calls he complains of stomach pains and wants her to come home to take care of him. The stomach pains are real, but the doctor can find no physical reason for them. Tommy's mother has recently remarried and Tommy feels left out. Tommy's pain is saying: "Something is wrong with me—please care about me." And mother feels guilty because her remarriage has "caused" her son's pains.

☐ Arthur, a noncustodial father whose ex-wife recently remarried, writes his fourteen-year-old daughter every week, telling her he loves her very much and wants to visit her. She refuses to answer his letters or see him (although she still loves him very much) because he walked out on her mother. She feels he walked out on her, too. She believes it is better not to trust any man—Mom's new husband may eventually walk out on them, too. The father feels guilty because his child rejects him. What can he ever do to make it up to her?

☐ Rachel feels guilty because she finds her new husband's kids unlikable; and John feels the same way about Rachel's children. Both feel they "should" like each other's children, and each feels guilty that they don't.

In a creative commitment, dilemmas such as these are openly acknowledged and discussed instead of hidden. A mutual sharing of pain and confusion will enable you to gain a more realistic understanding of the situation. Guilt often originates from the unrealistic expectations you had for the remarriage in the first place. When you substitute realistic possibilities for the fantasies, much of the guilt will vanish. Take the long view of how to improve relationships with your children and stepchildren. Your guilt will dissolve when you give up the belief that instant happiness is due you.

☐ Jo's guilt stems from her belief that anger makes her a "bad" stepmother. When Jo realizes that her stepdaughter may have been rude not because she disliked her, but because of her mixed feelings about the remarriage; and when Jo recognizes that the love between herself and her husband must be differentiated from her feelings about his children, then much of the guilt will vanish.

☐ Henry, the father who angered his two children, can demonstrate his love for them by becoming open about his needs and feelings and more aware of their needs and feelings.

☐ Ten-year-old Tommy will stop getting stomachaches when his mother gives him the security of her love. Greater verbal reassurance that she loves him now as much as she ever did before is required. More sensitive attention to Tommy's needs when she is at home with him and her new husband is indicated. Permitting him to express his pain and fear directly to her and his new stepfather, rather than indirectly through his stomachache, will help end his feeling of being uncared for and his mother's guilt over being a "bad" mother.

☐ When Arthur understands that "this too shall pass," his guilt will diminish. So long as he believes his daughter is rejecting him for life, his guilt will intensify. But if he keeps the lines of communication between them open, eventually she will respond. When her hurt lessens—and time indeed will lessen it—she will reconnect with her father she loves. Understanding his child's mixed feelings and the need for time to soothe her pain can lessen the burden of pain he is feeling.

☐ Rachel and her husband will stop feeling guilty when they acknowledge to themselves and to each other

Index